Judy Murrah's
Jacket Jackpot

Judy Murrah

Martingale®
& COMPANY

Judy Murrah's Jacket Jackpot
© 2003 by Judy Murrah

That Patchwork Place® is an imprint of
Martingale & Company®.

Martingale & Company
20205 144th Avenue NE
Woodinville, WA 98072-8478 USA
www.martingale-pub.com

Credits

President . . . . Nancy J. Martin
CEO . . . . Daniel J. Martin
Publisher . . . . Jane Hamada
Editorial Director . . . . Mary V. Green
Managing Editor . . . . Tina Cook
Technical Editor . . . . Barbara Weiland
Copy Editor . . . . Ellen Balstad
Design Director . . . . Stan Green
Illustrator . . . . Laurel Strand
Cover and Text Designer . . . Stan Green
Studio Photographer . . . . . . Brent Kane
Fashion Photographer . . . . . Pat Mercer

Mission Statement
Dedicated to providing quality products
and service to inspire creativity.

Library of Congress Cataloging-in-Publication Data

Murrah, Judy.
  Judy Murrah's jacket jackpot / Judy Murrah.
    p. cm.
  ISBN 1-56477-499-6
  1. Coats. 2. Vests. 3. Patchwork—Patterns.
4. Quilted goods. I. Title: Jacket jackpot.
II. Title.
  TT535.M882 2003
  746.46'0432—dc22

                                    2003016636

Printed in China
08 07 06 05 04   8 7 6 5 4 3 2

Dedication

I dedicate this book to motherhood! Writing a book is similar to the birthing process. And like a mother and her baby, there is a strong connection between the author and the finished book. However, this author-book relationship is not quite as strong as the connection I feel to my family. Being a mother has been and still is the most rewarding and the most important part of my life. As I completed this book and waited for the birth of my new granddaughter, Lindsey Cameron, I marveled at how my life has come full circle. My daughter, Holly, and her baby were uppermost in my mind as I worked on the projects. My stitches felt alive with love and joyful anticipation for the new life that was growing inside her. So here's to motherhood! It is the essence of all creativity!

Acknowledgments

My deepest gratitude goes to my editor and dear friend, Barbara Weiland. I call her a miracle worker. Without her way with words, her encouragement, and her support, this book would not have been written. I am always amazed at what she can do to turn my ideas and words into a beautiful book that makes sense to the reader.

I also owe thanks to the following people whose generosity and support helped this book become a reality:

Beatrice Steffek, my sewing angel, for her assistance in finishing the jackets and vests in this book.

The kind people and companies who supplied fabrics and notions for this book. They made it possible to turn my design dreams into the bright and colorful jackets and vests in this book. They include:

David Peha and Nancy Mahoney at Clothworks/Fabric Sales Co.; Donna Wilder of FreeSpirit; Billy Alper at Blank Textiles; Kaffe Fassett and Liza Prior Lucy with Westminster Fibers, Inc.; and Theresa Stelter of Hillcreek Designs.

Contents

Foreword

WHEN I FIRST MET JUDY MURRAH in the late spring of 1991, I was enchanted with her creativity. The vibrant and colorful jackets she wore every day at Quilt Market were the inspiration for her first book on wearables, *Jacket Jazz*. It was a privilege for me to edit *Jacket Jazz* and I loved working with Judy on the books that followed in quick succession. As the years passed and more books and patterns emerged, I continued to marvel at Judy's ability to design and create new and exciting jackets and vests. There was always something new in her work, along with the time-honored patchwork, beading, and stitchery techniques that are near and dear to her heart.

It has been a joy to work with Judy again, this time on *Judy Murrah's Jacket Jackpot*, another book full of her exuberant work. In these new jackets and vests, Judy focuses on creating less-complex projects with fewer techniques to cover the underlying garment foundation that she uses as her blank canvas.

Judy's generosity in sharing her work has inspired and touched the lives of thousands of quilters and sewers around the world, myself included. Once just her editor and now her friend, I am blessed to know her, to edit her work, and to continue to be inspired by her generous nature, her endless energy, and her unbridled creativity. Just as her work lights up the lives of many, her love, friendship, and beautiful smile light up my life. I hope making one of Judy's jackets will light up yours. Happy stitching!

—*Barbara Weiland*

5

Here We Go—Again!

JUDY MURRAH'S JACKET JACKPOT is my sixth book on wearables. When I sat down to write my first book, *Jacket Jazz*, I never dreamed that it would lead to writing five more books about one of my most favorite and creative pastimes!

Creating the vest and jacket projects for this book was a little like finding the "something old, something new" for a wedding. As I thought about my students' favorite projects, it was easy to select the most popular jacket and vest shapes from my previous books and patterns. Then I chose patchwork embellishments—some old and some new—to design the five new projects in this book for you to stitch from your favorite fabrics. Last but not least, I chose new fabrics from new fabric collections designed by many of the friends I have made over the years during my career as education director for Quilts, Inc., which produces successful international quilt markets and festivals each year. Now that the book is finished, I can't wait to see how you interpret these designs into vests and jackets that you love to wear.

Seeing my students succeed has been one of the most rewarding parts of my teaching and designing career. Creating and sharing my ideas in my books and classes has been a passion that continues to inspire and reward me in countless ways. I have made so many new friends around the world and right here at home. My life is enriched daily by those who share with me their love of patchwork and quilting in my classes and in my job. Although we are all unique, with very different lives and personal challenges, there is a thread of steel that connects us all in a wonderful circle of creativity.

I hope the projects and ideas in the pages that follow inspire you to create a garment you will love to wear. It would be fun to see photos of your finished projects so that the connecting thread remains strong and I can admire your creativity.

If you would like to participate in my next Mystery Jacket correspondence course, during which each student completes a jacket in five months, write to me at Judy Murrah, 109 Pasadena Dr., Victoria, Texas, 77904, or email me at judyjaz@attglobal.net. Happy stitching!

—*Judy Murrah*

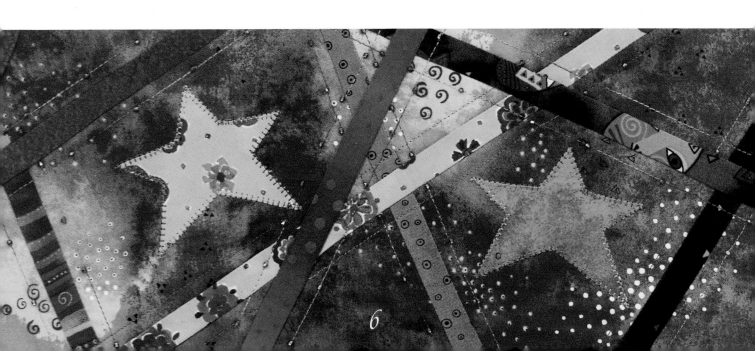

Let's Get Started

EACH PROJECT IN THIS BOOK features only four different patchwork techniques, making it faster and easier to sew than the more complex garments in my previous books. The kimono-style, loose-fitting jacket pattern has dropped shoulders, a banded neckline, and a front-edge finish. This simple style has proven to be a great backdrop for patchwork embellishments. It is easy to wear and flattering on all figures. The two classic-style vest patterns feature different lengths—one is long and the other is short.

There are two different jacket projects for you to try with the jacket pattern, plus another version without the sleeves—an easy vest to pop over a T-shirt or turtleneck. If you prefer vests, you can make the first two jackets without sleeves and finish the armhole as directed for "Vest One: Fantasia" (see page 43). The last two projects in the book are vests, comfortable to wear year 'round in any climate.

Each of the garments requires making a muslin foundation on which to build the patchwork designs (or you can use cotton flannel for the foundation for added warmth). A lining covers all the stitching on the wrong side of the foundation when you finish the jacket or vest.

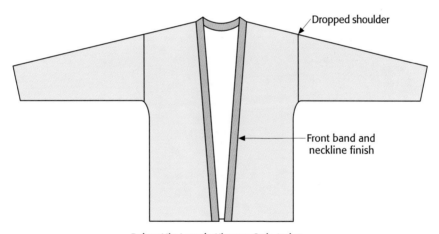

Below Hip-Length, Kimono-Style Jacket

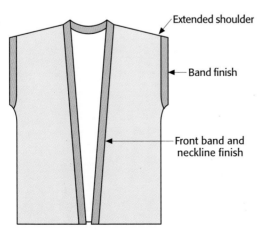

Below Hip-Length, Kimono-Style Vest

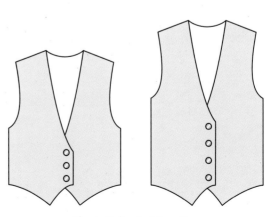

Classic Styling in 2 Lengths

PATTERN PIECE OVERVIEW AND SIZING

The vest and jacket pattern pieces are printed on the pattern pullouts and are multi-sized, with cutting lines marked for five sizes: Petite (6–8), Small (10–12), Medium (14–16), Large (18–20), and Extra-Large (22–24).

Sizing Chart

	Bust	Hip
Petite (6–8)	29"–32"	32"–34½"
Small (10–12)	33"–35½"	35½"–38"
Medium (14–16)	36"–38½"	38½"–40½"
Large (18–20)	39½"–42½"	41½"–44½"
Extra-Large (22–24)	43"–46"	45"–48"

The lengthen/shorten lines on the vest and jacket front and back pattern pieces make it easy to customize the length for your figure.

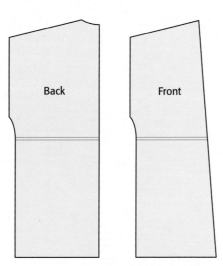

Lengthen or shorten at the double lines.

You can also adjust the jacket sleeve length. The jacket pattern is a dropped-shoulder style; the shoulder seam line will be approximately 4" below the outer edge of your shoulder. In addition, the sleeve has no hem allowance, just a ½"-wide seam allowance at the lower edge. Remember that if you use shoulder pads as recommended, the sleeve will be a bit shorter so it is essential to adjust the sleeve length (see below) before you cut the sleeves. Because the shoulder is dropped, the sleeve cap is flat, making it easy to set it into an open armhole—as you would for a sleeve in a classic shirt.

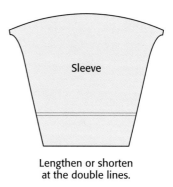

Lengthen or shorten at the double lines.

The jacket is loose fitting, with room in the sleeve, through the bustline, and at the full hip (7" below the waist). If you prefer a closer fit, you may want to use a smaller size than you're accustomed to sewing in more fitted styles.

Refer to the sizing chart to choose the pattern size that best corresponds to your body measurements. If you fall between sizes, choose the smaller size and test the fit as directed below:

1. Trace the front and back pattern pieces for your size onto pattern tracing paper or tissue paper. Mark the ½" seam lines at the shoulder, armhole, and underarm edges. Cut out the traced pieces.

2. Pin the front and back pieces together, positioning the pins along the seam line.

3. Try on the pinned pattern (and slip the shoulder pad in place if you are making a jacket). If the pattern is too large for your fit preference, unpin it, reposition the pieces over the master pattern pieces, and trace the next smaller size. Mark the seam lines and repin for a second test fitting.

4. To test the sleeve fit in your jacket, trace and cut out the sleeve pattern for the jacket size you have chosen. Mark the seam lines on the sleeve cap and underarms.

5. Pin the sleeve underarm seam, positioning the pins along the seam line.

6. Slip the pinned jacket body on with the shoulder pad. Then slip the pinned sleeve over your arm, overlapping the seam allowances at the shoulder seam. Check the sleeve length and adjust as needed using the lengthen/shorten lines on the pattern.

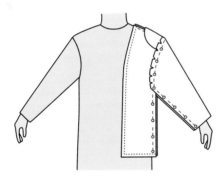

You can also adjust the fit once the patchwork pieces have been made and attached to the jacket foundation. Simply taper the side seams from the underarm down to the bottom

edge of the jacket. If you want the sleeve a little narrower at the wrists, taper the underarm seam, too.

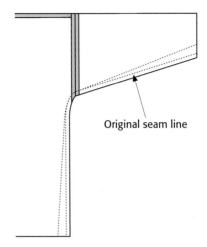

Original seam line

Taper side seams and underarm seam
for a closer fit at hip and cuff.

To test the vest fit, trace the front and back pieces, mark the seam lines, and pin together as shown for the jacket. Adjust the fit at the side seams. If needed, cut vest front and back wider at the side seams to fit over fuller tummy and hips in the longer version. Add width at the lower edge and taper back to the original cutting line at the underarm.

Add width,
tapering to nothing
at underarm.

NOTE: The vest pattern pieces provided are for "Vest Three: Dancing in the Cabin," which is the longer version. For "Vest Two: Patched Rhythms," shorten at the line indicated on the front and back pieces.

FABRIC SELECTION GUIDELINES

Paying careful attention to fabric designs, color contrast, and coordination is the key to creating visually exciting garments. If you follow my trademark recipe approach and the illustrated, step-by-step directions for creating the vests and jackets in this book, you are sure to be successful—even if this is your very first piece of wearable art. The following are some basic steps for selecting fabrics:

1. Choose the jacket or vest you want to make.

2. Make a shopping list—or take this book with you to your favorite fabric store. Many of the design elements in these projects require only ¼-yard or ½-yard cuts. You can use fat quarters for any fabric that requires ¼ yard. However, if you do use a fat quarter, you will need to cut the piece in half and sew the two strips together to make a piece that is 9" wide, like a standard ¼ yard is cut, before you proceed with the patchwork.

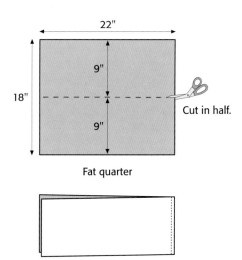

Fat quarter

Stitch ¼" from short ends.

3. At the store (or from your stash), pull fabrics that match the effect you want to create.

   • Follow the materials list carefully, referring to the photos to get a sense of the required color contrast.

• Consider the descriptions for the fabrics in the shopping list as you make your selections and look at the photos for ideas.

• For visual interest, include a variety of print types—small, medium-scale, large-scale, tone-on-tone, abstracts, florals, geometrics, conversational, and fabrics with the look of hand dyeing or watercolor effects.

• Remember that small prints often read as a solid from a distance; make sure you like the effect by grouping the fabrics and viewing them from a distance.

WINNING TIP

After you purchase your fabrics and determine how you will use them, attach snippets of each fabric to an index card. Label each fabric with the correct number and/or letter. (See the individual project instructions for fabric numbers and/or letters.) Keep this card handy as a visual reminder of your plan as you cut and make the patchwork pieces.

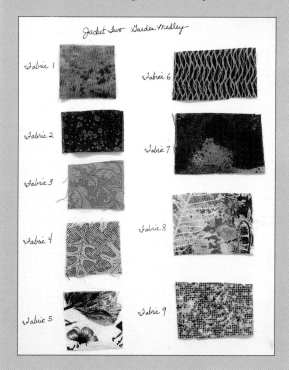

• Strive for contrast and/or visual interest in fabrics that will be used as backdrops for patchwork or in large areas, such as the back of the jacket "Jazz Squared" (see page 13).

• Stand back and look at the fabrics you've collected as a group to see if they work together. Squint to see if they blend well and the colors you want to pop out or dominate really do.

• Eliminate prints that look muddy, don't blend well, or seem too bright, too dull, too light, or too dark with the others. Replace those that don't work with new choices; then stand back and evaluate your choices again.

• Don't forget that you can always make fabric substitutions later if something just doesn't work the way you thought it would.

BASIC SUPPLIES

The following is a list of notions and tools you will need for the projects in this book:

• To trace the pattern pieces for your project from the pattern sheets provided, you will need pattern tracing paper or tissue paper.

• A rotary mat, cutter, and ruler are essential to accurate cutting.

• Some projects require trims for embellishing seams, piping edges, or adding texture and visual interest with couching. Look for trims that add a bit of contrast as they are often used to define seam lines or sections of the design.

• Lightweight fusible interfacing is essential for adding support to hemlines, vest necklines, and the jacket band. A lightweight knit, woven, or weft-insertion interfacing is preferable to stiffer nonwoven

interfacings (ask for these instead of the nonwoven types at your favorite fabric store). You will also need a press cloth and a copy of the manufacturer's fusing directions.

• Look for covered raglan-style or teardrop-shaped shoulder pads to add shoulder support and shaping to your finished jacket.

• You will need fusible web for some of the techniques. I prefer Steam-a-Seam 2; the Lite version is particularly nice because it isn't too stiff after fusing.

FABRIC PREPARATION AND CARE GUIDELINES

Because it is best to dry-clean embellished wearables, it is not necessary to preshrink the fabrics. Cotton fabrics that are not preshrunk have more body and are easier to handle—a bonus when it comes to making the patchwork pieces. Dry cleaning also ensures that colors will not run and trims will not shrink.

If your garment has beaded embellishments, ask the dry cleaner to clean and steam only; do not press. Keep dry cleaning to a minimum by spot cleaning your garment whenever necessary.

WINNING TIP

Take care of your jacket or vest to keep cleaning to a minimum. Periodic spot cleaning may be all that is required, since you will be wearing the garment over a blouse or shirt and it is lined as well. Washing is not recommended.

Jazz Squared

Front and Back Views

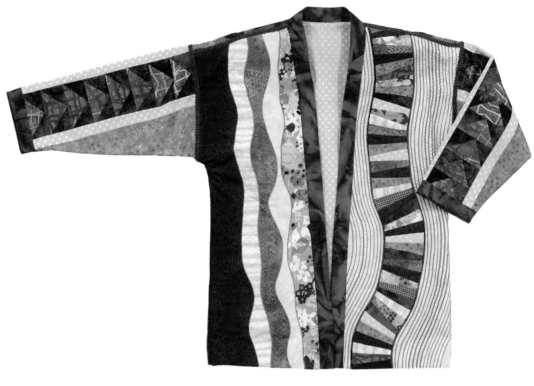

SHOPPING LIST

All yardage requirements listed are based on 44"-wide fabrics. You can use fat quarters for any fabric that requires ¼ yard if you prepare it for cutting as directed on page 10.

Basics

Jacket pattern: Pattern tracing paper or tissue paper and the pattern pullouts included with this book

Jacket foundation: 2½ to 3 yards of cotton flannel or muslin

Jacket lining: 2½ to 3 yards of cotton print or solid

Interfacing: ⅜ yard of lightweight fusible interfacing (woven, knit, or weft-insertion type)

Shoulder pads: Covered, raglan-style shoulder pads, ¼" to ½" thick

Patchwork Fabrics

For color group A, choose three strong coordinating prints in the same color family. Contrast is vital to make the design pop in this jacket. The fabrics in one of the three color groups must read as lighter than the prints in the others to create the necessary contrast.

¼ yard of fabric A1: medium-scale print for left front, right front, and back contrast band

¼ yard of fabric A2: medium-scale print for left front, right front, and back

½ yard of fabric A3: small-scale print (may read as a solid) for left front, left sleeve, right sleeve, and back

For color group B, the three prints should be coordinates with good contrast in small to medium scale. These fabrics should read as light in contrast to the other prints in your jacket.

¼ yard of fabric B1: small-scale print for left front, right front, and back

½ yard of fabric B2: medium-scale print for left front, right front, and back

½ yard of fabric B3: medium-scale print for left sleeve, right sleeve, left front, and back

For color group C, choose prints that contrast with color groups A and B. Some of the prints should include one of the colors found in color group A or B.

¼ yard of fabric C1: small-scale print (may read as a solid) for left front, right front, and back

½ yard of fabric C2: small-scale print (may read as a solid) for left sleeve, right sleeve, left front, and back

½ yard of fabric C3: medium-scale print for back, left sleeve, right sleeve, and left front

¼ yard of fabric C4: medium-scale print for left front and back

1 yard of fabric C5: large-scale, two-color print or tone-on-tone for lower back, left front, left sleeve, right sleeve, and front band

Notions and Special Supplies

- Template plastic

- 2½ yards of ½"- to 1"-wide decorative braid for covering seams

- 15 to 20 yards of narrow braid, yarn, or cord for couched trim on the left front and right front

- 3 yards of piping for left front and sleeve bottoms

- Rotary-cutting equipment: mat, ruler, and cutter

- Zipper or piping foot

- Optional: Cording presser foot for attaching couched trim

GETTING READY TO SEW

1. On pattern tracing or tissue paper, trace the jacket front, back, and sleeves for your size from the pattern pullouts in this book.

2. Cut the pieces from the lining and the foundation fabrics. Stay stitch the front and back neckline edges ⅜" from the raw edges. Set the lining pieces aside.

3. Cut 3"-wide strips of fusible interfacing and apply fusible interfacing to the wrong side of the foundation front, back, and sleeves.

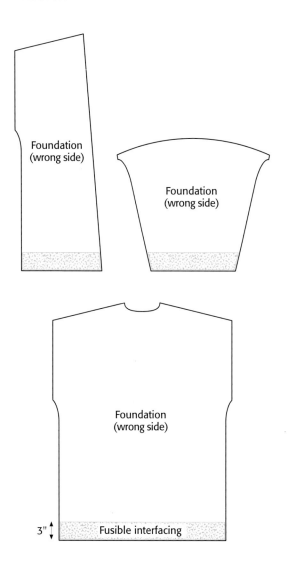

Foundation (wrong side)

Foundation (wrong side)

Foundation (wrong side)

3" Fusible interfacing

Construction at a Glance

Fill
(step 23, pages 20–21)

Fill
(step 15, page 26)

Square Dance
(pages 17–21)

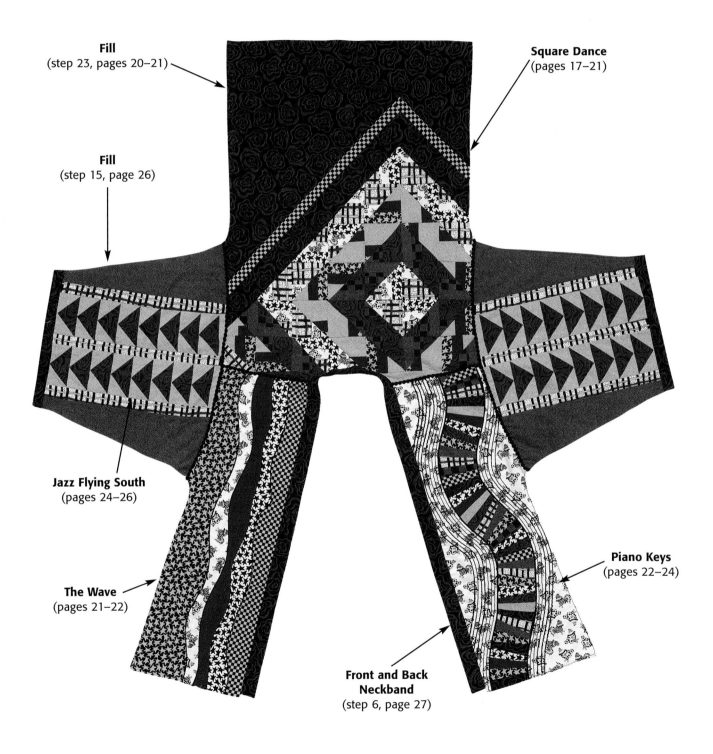

Jazz Flying South
(pages 24–26)

The Wave
(pages 21–22)

**Front and Back
Neckband**
(step 6, page 27)

Piano Keys
(pages 22–24)

IMPORTANT NOTES

For all patchwork, cut strips across the fabric width (selvage to selvage). If you are using fat quarters when the fabric requires ¼ yard, see the cutting and sewing illustration on page 10.

All patchwork seam allowances are ¼" wide. All garment construction seam allowances are ½" wide.

JACKET BACK: SQUARE DANCE

1. From each of fabrics A3, B3, and C3, cut 1 strip, 2½" wide.

2. From each of fabrics A2, B1, B2, C1, C2, and C4, cut 1 strip, 1½" wide.

3. Arrange the strips into sets in the following order:
   Strip set 1: A3, C1, A2
   Strip set 2: B3, B2, B1
   Strip set 3: C3, C4, C2

4. Sew the strips together and press the seams in one direction in each strip set.

Strip Set 1

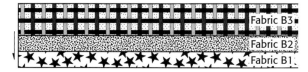

Strip Set 2

Strip Set 3

5. Place each strip set on the cutting mat with the 2½"-wide strip at the top. Cut each strip set into as many 4½" squares as possible, leaving them in place on the mat. Cut each square on the diagonal as shown, alternating the direction from square to square. Number the triangles as shown.

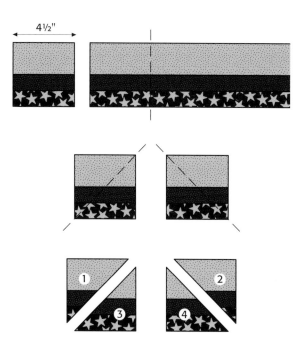

6. Pair a triangle 4 of strip set 2 with a triangle 3 of strip set 3. Sew the triangles together along the diagonal edge. Take care to match the seams. Press the seam toward the darker half of the resulting square. Pair a triangle 2 of strip set 2 with a triangle 1 of strip set 3. Sew the triangles together along the diagonal edge. Sew these two squares together carefully, following the diagram for placement. Press the seams in one direction.

7. In the same fashion, pair a triangle 1 of strip set 2 with a triangle 2 of strip set 3. Stitch and press. Pair a triangle 3 of strip set 2 with a triangle 4 of strip set 3. Stitch and press. Following the diagram, sew the resulting two blocks together and press the seams in one direction.

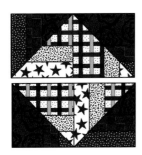

8. Position the block pairs as shown in the illustration, *but do not stitch them together.*

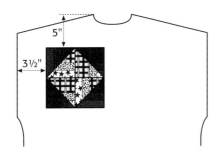

9. Place the block pairs on the right side of the back foundation near the left shoulder, following the diagram for correct placement. *Do not stitch anything in place on the foundation until directed.* You are preparing the patchwork rows.

10. Add four pairs of strip set 3 triangles to create a square on point.

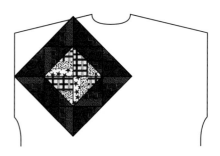

11. Add strip set 1 triangles beyond the strip set 3 triangles to continue the square shape. My sample has 16 triangles.

12. Follow with a round of strip set 2 triangles. As you reach the edges of the foundation, some triangles will extend beyond the foundation. My sample has 15 triangles.

WINNING TIP

Choose and place triangles randomly around the center square on point. The order of the 1, 2, 3, and 4 triangles is not important when adding these rounds.

13. Cover the remaining foundation above the square, out to the right shoulder, adding leftover strip-set 3 triangles first and following with strip-set 1 triangles. The design is now complete and ready to sew together into horizontal rows so that you can use the stitch-and-flip method of attaching them to the foundation. This method is described in the steps that follow.

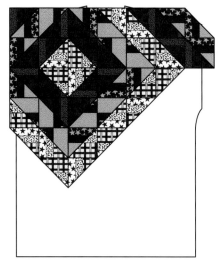

Pieces are positioned
but not yet stitched.

14. Beginning with the upper row of triangles, sew the pieces together in rows. Press the seams in opposite directions from row to row. You will have a total of six patchwork rows.

15. Pin row 1 to the foundation. The upper raw edge of row 1 should be at the neckline raw edge.

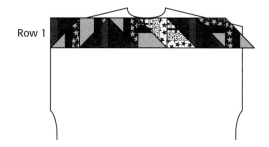

Row 1

16. With right sides together and raw edges even, pin row 2 to the bottom edge of row 1. Stitch both strips to the foundation ¼" from the patchwork raw edges. Flip row 2 down onto the foundation and press. Pin in place.

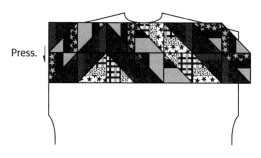

Press.

17. Add rows 3–6 in the same manner. Some of the foundation will be exposed at both shoulder edges.

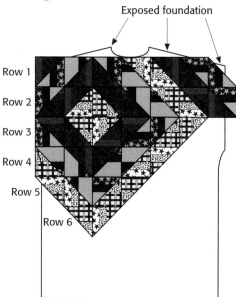

Exposed foundation

Row 1
Row 2
Row 3
Row 4
Row 5
Row 6

18. Trim excess row 2 even with foundation edges at right armhole edge.

19. Cut a strip from one of the fabrics in color group A 1" wider than the exposed foundation at the left shoulder. Use the stitch-and-flip method to attach the strip to the patchwork and foundation. Repeat at the right shoulder, using strips from a fabric in color group B at the outer corner as needed and following with a strip from color group C at the shoulder edge.

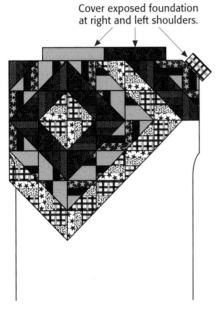

Cover exposed foundation at right and left shoulders.

20. From fabric C5, cut a 3"-wide strip. Use the stitch-and-flip method to attach the strip to the right edge of the patchwork. Press and pin in place.

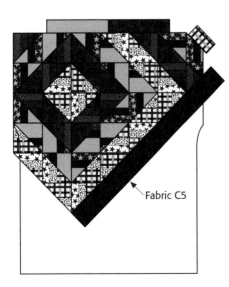

Fabric C5

21. Repeat step 19 on the left edge of the patchwork.

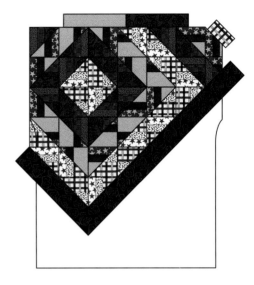

22. Cut a 1½"-wide strip of fabric A1. Use the stitch-and-flip method to attach the strip to the right edge. Press and pin in place. Repeat at the left edge.

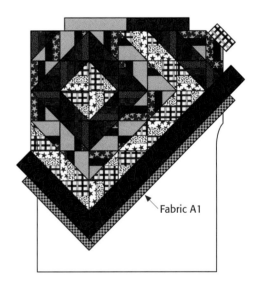

Fabric A1

23. Use the stitch-and-flip method to sew fabric C5 to the lower-right edge of the patchwork panel. Repeat at the left edge of the patchwork to cover the remainder of the foundation. Trim excess fabric and patchwork even with the outer edges of the foundation. Stitch ⅛" from the raw edges. Set the completed back aside.

RIGHT FRONT: THE WAVE

1. From each of fabrics A1, B1, B2, and C1, cut a 3"-wide strip. Measure the front foundation at its longest point and use this measurement for the length of the strips.

2. Position a fabric A1 strip face up on the rotary-cutting mat with a fabric B1 strip, overlapping it by 1" at the long edge. Use a rotary cutter to cut a softly flowing curve through both fabric layers at once. Discard the smaller strips of fabric.

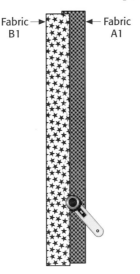

3. Flip the strips over and use a pencil or marking pen to make ¼"-long marks across both cut edges at each of the curves for matching purposes.

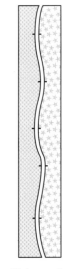

Make marks at curves for matching.

4. With right sides together, raw edges even, and marks matching, use a few pins to hold the two curved edges together—a bit like you would pin together the pieces of a curved patchwork block such as Drunkard's Path. Don't fret. Just coax the edges together as you sew. Stitch slowly to avoid puckers and sew ¼" from the raw edges. Press the seam to one side.

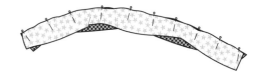

5. Repeat steps 2–4 with strips of fabric C1 and B2. Overlap fabric C1 on the long edge of fabric B1 and fabric B2 on the long edge of C1.

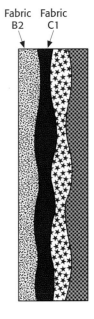

6. Position the patchwork on the right side of the right-front foundation. Then determine the width of fabric A2 needed to cover the remaining foundation to the outer edge, plus 1½". Cut a strip to this width and follow steps 1–4 to add this strip to the wave panel. (See step 7 illustration below.)

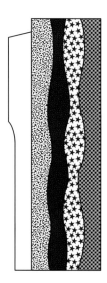

7. Pin the completed wave panel to the right side of the right-front foundation. Place fabric A1 at the center front edge. Trim excess fabric even with the foundation edges. Stitch ⅛" from the outer raw edges.

8. Position decorative cord or trim along each seam line and zigzag stitch over it to couch it in place. Use your all-purpose presser foot, or attach a couching-braiding foot if available. Adjust the zigzag stitch to clear the width of the trim, and lengthen the stitch. Pull about 1" of decorative trim behind the foot and begin to stitch, zigzagging over the trim and holding it taut in front of the foot. It is important after completing each row to tug gently on the right-front piece to relax any puckers that may have developed while you were stitching.

**Zigzag over cord
to couch next to seam lines.**

LEFT FRONT: PIANO KEYS

1. Use the front pattern piece to cut a left front from fabric B2.

2. Place the piece face up on top of the left-front foundation with raw edges even. Stitch ⅛" from the raw edges.

3. With the exception of fabric B2, cut a 1½"-wide strip from each of the fabrics in all three color groups.

4. Make a template using the pattern on pull-out 2B. Use it to trace and cut a total of 40 wedges from the strips you just cut. You may also cut wedges from any of the scraps from this project.

5. Beginning at the lower edge of the foundation, arrange the wedges in a softly curving design. Alternate the wide and narrow ends as needed to create the desired shape. Play with the color placement.

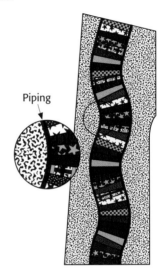

Fabric B2

6. When pleased with the design and color placement, sew the wedges together in the desired order, *separate from the fabric-covered foundation,* and press the seams in one direction. Periodically place the patchwork on the background to check the curve; it will probably be necessary to add another wedge here and there to maintain the desired shape and the correct length because you lose some of the original length in the seaming.

7. With raw edges even, stitch the piping to the patchwork strip. If you have a piping foot, use it for this step. If not, adjust the zipper foot so that you can stitch as close to the piping cord as possible.

8. Turn under the raw edges of the piping and the seam allowance so that the piping cord lies along the edge of the strip. Press. Add piping to the remaining raw edge of the strip in the same manner.

9. Pin the piped strip to the left front. Using thread to match the piping, stitch in the ditch between the piping cord and the strip. Use your zipper foot for this step. Press.

Piping

10. Arrange yarn, cord, or narrow trim on the background fabric ¼" from the long edges of the piped patchwork. Couch as directed in step 8 on page 22 for the right front.

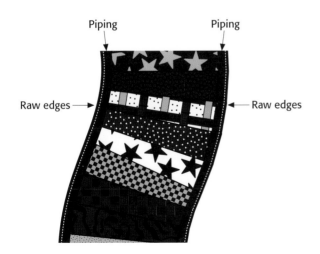

Piping   Piping

Raw edges →   ← Raw edges

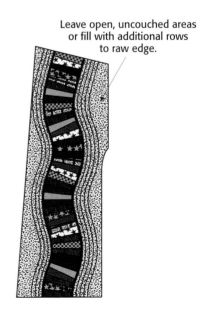

Leave open, uncouched areas or fill with additional rows to raw edge.

11. Continue adding rows of couching on each side of the piano-key strip (five or more rows). Use the width of your presser foot as a gauge for the distance between the rows.

NOTE: If the jacket fabric tends to pucker and pull up during the couching, give it a tug after stitching each row to smooth it out and prevent a permanently puckered front when it is finished. If you wish, add more couched rows until you reach the raw edges so that the entire background is covered with trim.

SLEEVES: JAZZ FLYING SOUTH

1. From fabric C3, cut a 5¼"-wide strip for the main triangles. Crosscut the strip into eight squares, each 5¼" x 5¼".

2. From fabric A3, cut two 2⅞"-wide strips across the fabric. Cut a third strip, 2⅞" x 12". Crosscut the strips into thirty 2⅞" background squares. On the wrong side of each square, draw a diagonal line from one corner to the opposite corner.

3. Stack the squares in groups of five or six. Make sure the marked lines are all placed in the same direction. Cut off a ½" triangle at one corner, making sure you are cutting across a corner that is intersected by the diagonal line. To make this easy, trace the corner cutting pattern on pullout 2B onto template plastic. Tuck the template around the corner of the stacked squares as shown and cut.

4. With right sides together and the cutoff corners facing toward the center, pin two small squares to a large C3 square. Machine stitch ¼" away from the marked line on both sides.

Stitch on both sides
of marked line.

5. Cut on the marked line.

Cut apart.

6. Press the resulting small background triangles away from the main triangle in each of the units.

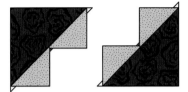

Press small triangles out.

7. With right sides together and the cutoff corner toward the center seam line, place one small square on each unit from step 6. Stitch ¼" away from the marked line on both sides. For quick chain piecing, stitch along one side of the line on all pieces and then stitch along the remaining side. (See "Winning Tip" on page 24.)

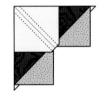

Add one more square.

8. Cut on the marked lines and press the small triangles away from the main triangle. Cut away the small triangles of seam allowance that extend at the corners and the point of each unit. This step yields two flying-geese units. Repeat for a total of 32 flying-geese units (16 for each sleeve).

Cut apart and press.
Make 32.

9. Arrange the flying-geese units in four rows of eight units each. Sew the units together in rows and press the seams toward the flying-geese points. Cut and sew a 1½" x 4½" strip of fabric A3 to the upper edge of each row. The geese may fly south, pointing to your wrist, or north, pointing to your shoulder, if you prefer. Press the seam toward the triangles.

Make 4.

WINNING TIP

Stitch accurately, taking care not to stitch across the tips of the large triangles.

10. From fabric B3, cut three strips, each 1½" wide. From these strips, cut six strips, each the length of the flying-geese rows.

11. Fold each sleeve foundation in half lengthwise and press to mark the center. Open the sleeve.

12. Center one strip over the crease in each sleeve foundation and pin in place.

13. Add a row of flying-geese units to each side of the center strip, using the stitch-and-flip method described for the patchwork back. Press and pin in place.

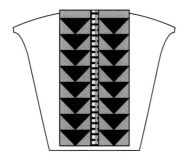

14. Add the remaining fabric B3 strips to the outer edges of the flying-geese rows in the same manner.

15. Use the stitch-and-flip method to add pieces of fabric C2 to cover the remaining foundation on each side of the flying-geese rows.

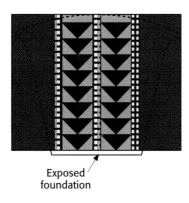

Exposed foundation

16. Cut a strip of fabric C5 to cover the exposed foundation at the bottom of each sleeve. Use the stitch-and-flip method to attach the strips to the sleeve foundations. Press and pin in place. Stitch ⅛" from all raw edges.

ASSEMBLING THE JACKET

Note that jacket-assembly seam allowances are ½" wide.

1. With right sides together, stitch the jacket shoulder seams and press open.

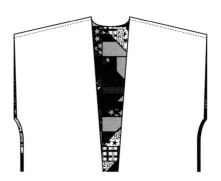

Stitch shoulder seams.

2. With right sides facing out, center decorative braid over the shoulder seam lines. Stitch in place.

3. With right sides together, stitch a sleeve to each armhole. Press the seams open and turn the garment right side out. Center decorative braid over the armhole seam lines and stitch in place.

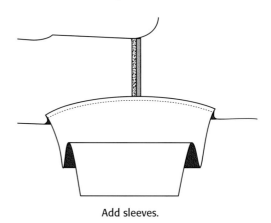

Add sleeves.

4. With right sides together, stitch the side seams, continuing to the bottom edge of the sleeves. Press the seams open.

5. Assemble the jacket lining in the same manner, excluding the braid trim. Turn under and press ¼" at the bottom edge of each sleeve lining.

6. For the neckband, cut two 3½"-wide strips of fabric C5 the width of the fabric.

7. Cut two strips of lightweight fusible interfacing that are the same length as the neckband strips but only 3¼" wide. Center each one on the wrong side of a neckband strip and fuse, following the manufacturer's directions.

8. Sew the two neckband strips together at one short end, using a ¼"-wide seam. Press the seam open.

9. Fold the band in half lengthwise with wrong sides together and press.

10. With the seam in the band positioned at the neckline center back and all raw edges even, pin the band to the jacket back neckline and front edges. Trim the excess band even with the jacket lower edge.

Trim excess band
even with lower edge.

11. To finish the band ends, unpin the lower ends for a few inches so that you can open them and turn them back on themselves with right sides together. Stitch ½" from the bottom raw edges. Trim the seam to ¼", clip the corner, and turn the band right side out again.

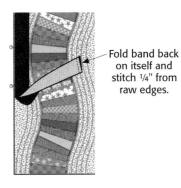

Fold band back on itself and stitch ¼" from raw edges.

12. Pin the band ends to the jacket and stitch the band in place ⅜" from the raw edges.

Finished ends of band
½" above jacket lower edge

FINISHING THE JACKET

1. Pin piping to the bottom edge of each sleeve, overlapping the ends as shown. Stitch close to the piping cord. Turn the seam allowance to the inside so that piping lies along the lower sleeve edge.

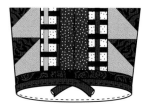

2. *With right sides together,* stitch the lining to the jacket ½" from the outer edges. Leave an 8"-long opening at the bottom edge of the center back for turning. Trim the seam to ¼". Turn right side out, pushing the lining sleeves into the jacket sleeves. Press, making sure the lining doesn't peek or roll out to the jacket right side at the outer finished edges. Press.

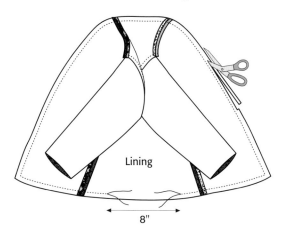

3. Turn in the seam allowances at the opening at the bottom edge of the jacket. Slipstitch the opening closed.

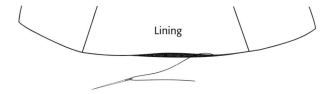

4. Turn the sleeves with the lining side out. Position the folded edge of the lining over the piping seam at the lower edge of the sleeve. Slipstitch the lower edge of the sleeve lining to the sleeve.

5. Tack the shoulder pads in place on the inside of the jacket.

JACKET TWO
Garden Melody

Front and Back View

SHOPPING LIST

All yardage requirements listed are based on 44"-wide fabrics. You can use fat quarters for any fabric that requires ¼ yard if you prepare it for cutting as directed on page 10.

Basics

Jacket pattern: Pattern tracing paper or tissue paper and pattern pullouts included with this book

Jacket foundation: 2½ to 3 yards of cotton flannel or muslin

Jacket lining: 2½ to 3 yards of cotton print or solid

Interfacing: ⅜ yard of lightweight fusible interfacing (woven, knit, or weft-insertion type)

Shoulder pads: Covered, raglan-style shoulder pads, ¼" to ½" thick

Patchwork Fabrics

To make the bargello patchwork as vivid as possible, choose fabrics with light and dark contrast in two or three color families. It may help to choose a larger, multicolored print first and then choose fabrics in the same colors featured in the print. For visual interest, choose an assortment of prints. For example, choose a multicolored print, a plaid, a tone-on-tone print or hand-dyed print, a medium print, a small print, and a solid color for interesting variety. You will need a total of nine fabrics.

Fabric 1: 1 yard of solid or tone-on-tone print for neckband, flower stem appliqués, left front, back, left sleeve, and right sleeve

Fabric 2: 1 yard of multicolored print or tone-on-tone print for lower back, left front, right front, left sleeve, and right sleeve

Fabric 3: ¼ yard of solid or tone-on-tone print for tulip appliqués and patchwork areas on back, left sleeve, and right sleeve

Fabric 4: ½ yard of solid or small print for left front, back, left sleeve, and right sleeve

Fabric 5: ¼ yard of multicolored print for back, left sleeve, and right sleeve

Fabric 6: ⅓ yard of small print for posy appliqués, right front, left sleeve, right sleeve, and back

Fabric 7: ½ yard of solid or tone-on-tone print for left sleeve, right sleeve, left front, right front, and back

Fabric 8: ½ yard of solid or print for right front, left sleeve, right sleeve, and leaf appliqués

Fabric 9: ½ yard of multicolored print on light background for right front, left front, and back

Notions and Special Supplies

- Template plastic

- Paper-backed fusible web

- 5 yards of braid or other trim to embellish seams

- 3½ yards of piping for neckband and sleeve edging

- 16 to 24 buttons (assorted sizes) for appliqué embellishment

- Rotary-cutting equipment: mat, ruler, and cutter

- Zipper or piping foot

- Optional: Glue stick, ½" bias tape maker

Construction at a Glance

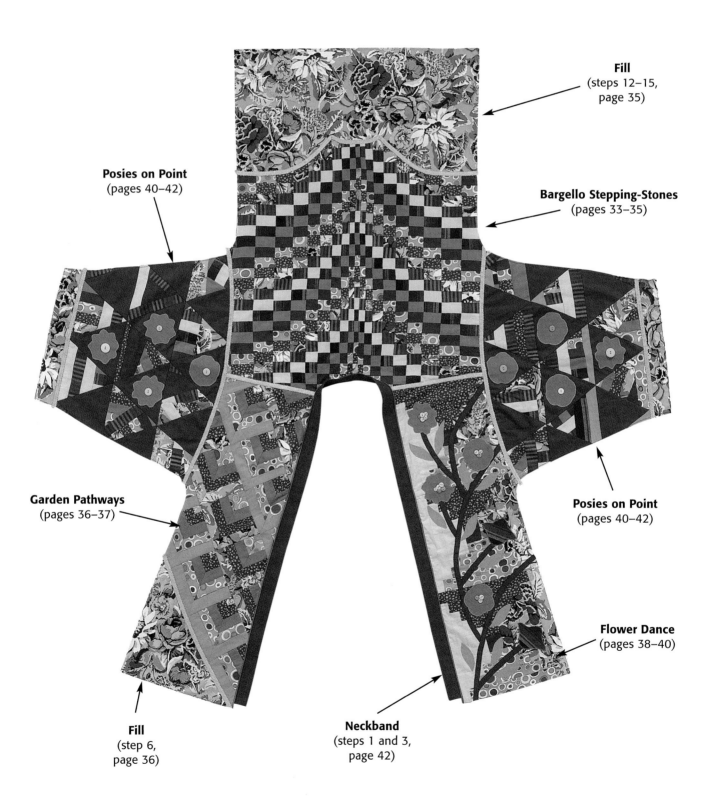

Fill
(steps 12–15,
page 35)

Posies on Point
(pages 40–42)

Bargello Stepping-Stones
(pages 33–35)

Garden Pathways
(pages 36–37)

Posies on Point
(pages 40–42)

Fill
(step 6,
page 36)

Neckband
(steps 1 and 3,
page 42)

Flower Dance
(pages 38–40)

GETTING READY TO SEW

1. On pattern tracing or tissue paper, trace the jacket front, back, and sleeves for your size from the pattern pullouts in this book.

2. Cut the pieces from the lining and the foundation fabrics. Stay stitch the front and back neckline edges ⅜" from the raw edges. Set the lining pieces aside.

3. Apply fusible interfacing to the wrong side of the foundation front, back, and sleeves (see illustration on page 15).

IMPORTANT NOTES

For all patchwork, cut strips across the fabric width (selvage to selvage). If you are using fat quarters when the fabric requires ¼ yard, see the cutting and sewing illustration on page 10.

All patchwork seam allowances are ¼" wide. All garment construction seam allowances are ½" wide.

JACKET BACK: BARGELLO STEPPING-STONES

1. From all but fabric 8, cut three strips, each 1½" wide, and arrange the strips in color families (similar colors). You should have three identical strip sets of eight strips each.

2. Beginning at the top of your strip-set arrangement, number the strips from 1 to 8. Sew the strips together in numerical order to make three strip sets. Press all seams in one direction. Sew the strip sets together, maintaining the color order.

Press. The finished strip unit should measure approximately 24" x 42".

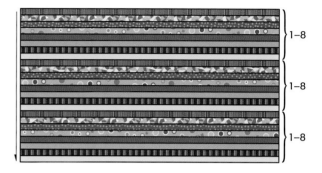

3. Fold the strip-pieced unit in half, right sides together. Beginning at the center of the folded strip unit, align the raw edges of the first and last strips to create a long tube; stitch. Read "Winning Tip" on page 34 if you are having difficulty aligning the edges.

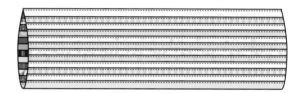

4. Using your rotary-cutting equipment, cut the tube into rings. Cut the first ring 1" wide. Cut two each of the following widths: 1¼", 1½", 1¾", 2", 2¼", 2½", 2¾", and 3". You will have a total of 17 rings and there will be a piece of tube left over. Cut this piece into two more rings of the widest width possible to match one of the previously cut widths. For example, if there is a 4¼"-long piece of the tube remaining, cut two 2"-wide rings and group them with the other 2" rings.

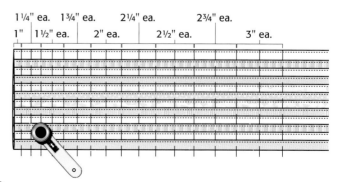

33

WINNING TIP

When folded in half in preparation for stitching, the strip-pieced tube should lie perfectly flat from the center point out with raw edges even. However, it may not lie flat along the entire length due to inaccuracies in cutting, stitching, and pressing. If it doesn't, it is essential to stitch *only* the center section where the edges do match and the bottom fold lies perfectly flat.

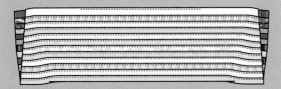

Cut strips from the stitched section only, as directed in step 4. Then realign the raw edges of the remaining sections of the strip piecing and stitch. The section that was causing the misalignment will be cut off before you cut the next series of strips. Cut a new straight edge on the tube.

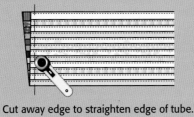

Cut away edge to straighten edge of tube.

5. Open a seam (it doesn't matter which one) of the 1"-wide ring by tugging gently at each side to loosen the stitches. Place the strip right side up on a flat surface or your design wall. Make sure the seams are pressed toward you (or toward the floor on a design wall). This strip is the center of the bargello design.

6. Identify the uppermost fabric in the 1"-wide bargello strip. Then find the same fabric in the 1¼"-wide rings. Move one strip down and open the seam in each ring, making sure that the seams are still pressed toward you. This means that the second fabric in the 1"-wide strip will be at the top of the 1¼"-wide strips. Position one of these strips at each side of the center strip with top edges even. Refer to the illustration with step 8 below.

7. Repeat step 6 with each of the remaining sets of rings, moving one strip down each time you open the seam of a new ring width. The ring must always be positioned so that the seam allowances are pressed toward you before you choose the seam to open (to keep the color sequencing intact).

8. After opening and positioning all of the strips, double-check the design to make sure that it is symmetrical on each side of the center.

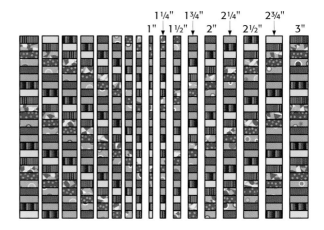

9. Pick up the strips from left to right, one at a time, and stack them in order. Place a pin in the upper corner of the strip on top of the stack to remind yourself not to sew a strip to that edge.

10. Stitch the strips together in order, using ¼"-wide seams. There is no need to pin to match the patchwork. Simply manipulate it at each seam to make it match the best you can. Your eye will see the design, not the accuracy in piecing.

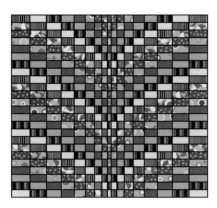

11. Lay the back foundation piece on a flat surface. Place the completed bargello on the back foundation, aligning the bargello with the shoulder seam, and pin in place. Trim the edges even with the foundation along the shoulders and neckline. *If the patchwork is not wide enough to cover the width of the back,* add a strip of multicolored fabric to both outer edges of the patchwork. Stitch ⅛" from the edges.

12. Trace the lower-back pattern from pullout 2B. Fold fabric 2 in half with selvages even. Place the fabric pattern along the fold line at one end of the fabric, cut the upper curved edge only, and extend it to the selvages.

13. Remove the pattern piece and place the fabric on the back foundation. Position it on top of the bargello as low as you can without the foundation showing. Pin in place along the curved edge (see "Construction at a Glance" on page 32). Trim any excess lower-back fabric even with the back foundation at the lower and side seam edges.

14. With pins still in place at the upper edge of fabric 2, trim the bargello lying underneath fabric 2 even with the curved edge. Remove the leftover bargello pieces and set them aside to use later for the sleeve patchwork.

15. Zigzag stitch the lower edge of the bargello and the upper edge of fabric 2 in place. Cover the raw edges with braid trim and stitch in place. Then stitch ⅛" from the outer edges of fabric 2.

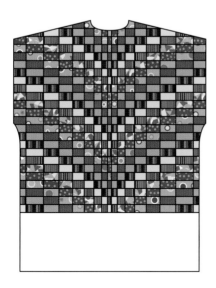

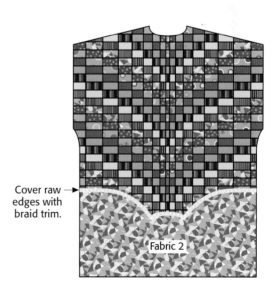

Cover raw edges with braid trim.

Fabric 2

RIGHT FRONT: GARDEN PATHWAYS

1. From each of fabrics 2, 6, 7, 8, and 9, cut two 1½"-wide strips.

2. Arrange and sew the strips into two identical strip sets in the following fabric order: 2, 7, 6, 9, 8. Press the seams in one direction (the same in both strip sets).

3. Cut each strip set into seven 5½" squares. Leave the squares in position on the cutting mat.

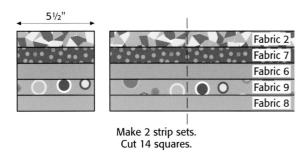

Make 2 strip sets.
Cut 14 squares.

4. Cut each square diagonally into two triangles, reversing the cutting direction across the strip as shown.

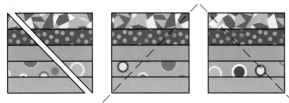

Cut into triangles, zigzag fashion.

5. Make 10 chevron squares by sewing together mirror-image triangles. You will have five of block A and five of block B. Press the seams in one direction. Clip off and discard the small triangles that extend

at the corners of each block. Save the remaining pieced triangles to use later.

Block A
Make 5.

Block B
Make 5.

6. Measure the length of the lower back (fabric 2) band at the side seam and mark this length at the side seam edge on the right-front foundation. Draw a line from this mark to the lower front-edge corner. Cover the lower area with a piece of fabric 2. Pin the fabric in place and trim even with the foundation. Stitch ⅛" from all raw edges.

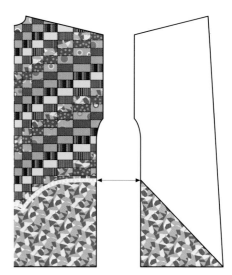

Fabric 2 matches at side seam.

7. Position a triangle that matches block B along the front edge of the foundation. Make sure fabric 8 is at the bottom along the edge of fabric 2. Add enough blocks to cover the foundation out to the side seam at the underarm. Sew the triangle and the blocks together and press the seams in one direction. Position the strip on the foundation. *The bottom edge should overlap fabric 2 by ⅛".* Pin the strip in place and trim the outer edges even with the foundation edges as needed; save the large cutaway pieces. Stitch the strip in place on the foundation. Cover the raw edges with braid trim and stitch in place.

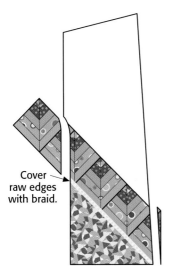

Cover raw edges with braid.

Trim excess even with foundation.

8. Using block A squares and a triangle that matches block A at the front edge with fabric 2 at the bottom, arrange the next row of pieces. Line the pieces up with the previous squares. Sew the squares and triangle together and press.

9. Place the second row face down on the first row of blocks. Make sure the raw edges and seam lines match. Stitch ¼" from the raw edges to attach the row to the foundation. Flip the row onto the foundation and press. Pin the row in place. Trim the excess even with the foundation.

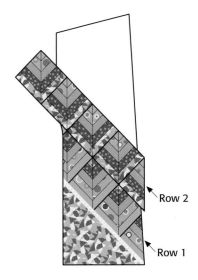

Row 2

Row 1

10. Continue in the same manner to complete rows 3 and 4 and cover the foundation. It may be necessary to piece another square to complete a row. If necessary, use cutaway pieces or a partial triangle, or cut fabric strips and flip and sew in place to cover any exposed foundation. Stitch ⅛" from all remaining raw edges.

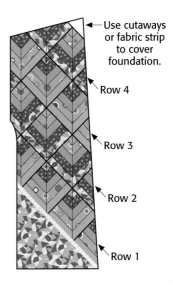

Use cutaways or fabric strip to cover foundation.

Row 4

Row 3

Row 2

Row 1

LEFT FRONT: FLOWER DANCE

1. Measure and mark the foundation with horizontal lines to divide it into three equal parts.

2. From fabric 1, cut three 2" squares for the Log Cabin block centers.

3. From each of fabrics 2, 4, 7, and 9, cut two strips, each 1½" wide.

4. Make three Log Cabin blocks (modified Courthouse Steps pattern), beginning with the 2" squares at the center. Add a strip of fabric 7 to one edge of the square, and a strip of fabric 2 to the adjacent edge. Press the seams away from the center square.

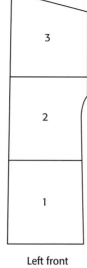

Left front

WINNING TIP

To speed up the process, use chain piecing as you add each round of strips. Butt the squares together. Cut the pieces apart, trimming the strips even with the edges of the previous round, and then press the seams away from the center square.

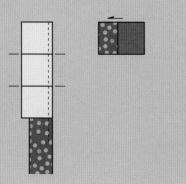

5. After adding fabric 2, add a strip of fabric 9, followed by a strip of fabric 4. Continue adding strips around the block in the same progression until you have added four strips of each color to each block.

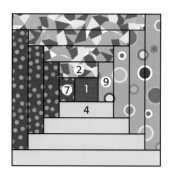

Make 3 blocks with
4 rounds of each color.

6. Position the completed block in the bottom third of the foundation. Make sure the outer edge of the last fabric 4 strip is at the foundation-front raw edge and the top of the block is aligned with the dividing line you drew. If the block is not large enough to cover the foundation from the dividing line to the bottom raw edge, add another strip of fabric 7 to the upper edge of the block. If it is not large enough to cover the foundation out to the side seam, add strips of fabric 2 until it is. Pin the block in place and trim it even with the foundation as needed.

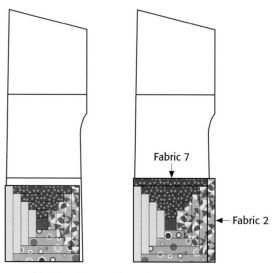

Fabric 7

Fabric 2

Add strips above and to right of block
to cover foundation.

7. Stitch and flip the remaining blocks in place on the foundation and trim as needed. Stitch and flip one or more strips of fabric 7 at the top edge of the upper block to cover the foundation completely. Stitch ⅛" from the raw edges.

Add strips of fabric 7 as needed to cover foundation.

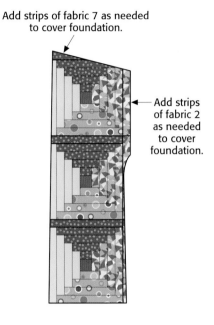

Add strips of fabric 2 as needed to cover foundation.

8. For flower stems, cut two 1"-wide strips from fabric 1. Turn under and press ¼" on each long edge of each strip.

WINNING TIP

I use a ½" bias tape maker to turn under the strip edges quickly and evenly.

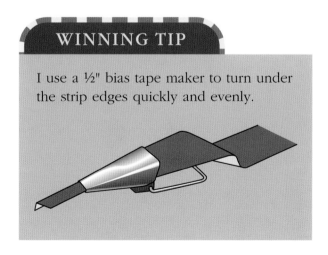

9. Referring to the jacket photo on page 32, arrange the strips to create a vine for the flowers and leaves—or create your own vine design. Arrange the vine so that at least one stem connects at the side seam to the back lower band. The other stems may end at the armhole edge if desired. Pin the vines in place and edgestitch along both turned edges using matching thread.

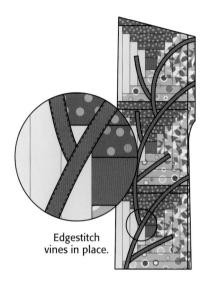

Edgestitch vines in place.

10. Using the leaf and flower template patterns on pullout 2B, make templates and trace 15 leaves, 11 posies, and two tulips onto the paper side of fusible web. Leave at least ½" between motifs. Cut the shapes out, leaving excess paper around each one.

11. Position the posies on the wrong side of fabric 6. Make sure the paper side is facing you and then fuse. Follow the manufacturer's directions for fusing. Allow to cool. Cut out the posies on the lines. Set eight posies aside for the sleeves. In the same manner, fuse and cut out the tulips from fabric 3 and the leaves from fabric 8.

12. Pin the tulips, posies, and leaves to the stems as desired (see jacket photo on page 32). It's not necessary to use all of the leaves. One by one, remove the pins, remove the paper backing from the appliqué, and fuse in place. Follow the manufacturer's directions for fusing.

13. Using a contrasting-color thread and your favorite machine appliqué stitch, stitch around the outer edges of each appliqué. To turn the corner at the point of a leaf, stop stitching with the needle in the jacket patchwork (not in the appliqué). Raise the presser foot and pivot the fabric into position. Lower the foot and continue stitching.

14. Press the completed front. Sew one or several buttons to the center of each posy.

WINNING TIP

I often work out my design ideas on paper if I'm out of town and away from my quilting studio. If I'm home in my studio, I work them out in fabric. I love to use up leftover fabric strips and to work with the equilateral triangle shape. The patchwork on the sleeves combines two of the things I love to do when bringing my designs to life.

SLEEVES: POSIES ON POINT

1. Make an equilateral triangle template by tracing the pattern on pullout 2B, unless you have an equilateral triangle ruler that will work.

2. Cut two 6"-wide strips of fabric 1. Using the template or your triangle ruler, cut 22 to 24 (for larger sizes) triangles from the strips.

3. Salvage strips for the patchwork from what's left of all the fabrics you used for the other patchwork in this jacket. Do you have some strips that are already pieced together? Do you have some extra strips that are not yet sewn to others? Set these to one side. Also look at the larger pieces of leftover fabrics. Is there an odd-shaped piece of fabric hanging off one or more ends? Trim away the odd-shaped piece and cut it into 1½"-wide strips to neaten up the piece. (Put the larger leftover pieces that you've neatened into your stash when you finish the sleeves.)

4. Arrange the salvaged strips in rows on a flat surface, beginning with the longest strip at the bottom and the shortest strip at the top.

5. Sew the two longest strips together, off-setting the shorter strip by ½". Continue adding strips in this manner, offsetting each one so that you create "stairsteps" at one end. Stitch enough strips together to make a strip unit that measures 6" wide (or slightly wider) and *at least* 6" high. Cut one or more equilateral triangles (as many as possible) from the strip unit, alternating the triangle as shown.

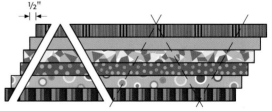

Alternate the triangle cutting template.

6. Continue strip piecing leftovers in this fashion to cut more triangles. If leftovers from a previous strip unit are large enough, add them to a strip unit. It is not necessary for all strips to be positioned in the same direction in these strip units. You will need approximately 20 pieced triangles.

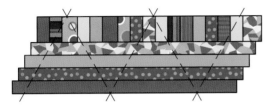

Some pieces may be vertical.

7. Draw a line on the right side of each sleeve foundation 2" above the bottom edge. Fold each sleeve foundation in half lengthwise and crease to mark the center. Open each one and place face up on your work surface.

8. Arrange pieced and plain triangles along the line, placing a plain fabric 1 triangle on point over the center crease.

9. Stitch the triangles together and press the seams in one direction. Reposition on the sleeve foundation at the 2" mark and pin in place. Trim away excess fabric even with the foundation at the underarm edges.

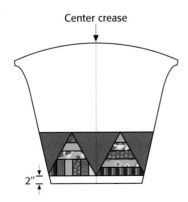

Center crease

2"

10. At the bottom edge of the triangle strip, stitch and flip a 2½"-wide piece of fabric 2. Trim even with the foundation edges. If you want, add a braid trim to the seam line, taking care not to cover and cut off the points of the triangles.

11. Repeat steps 8 and 9 to create triangle row 2. Stitch and flip to attach it to the upper edge of the first row on the foundation.

12. Repeat to add a third row of triangles.

13. If necessary, stitch and flip a strip of fabric 1 to the upper edge of row 3 to cover any exposed foundation. Trim even with the foundation edges.

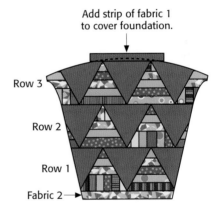

Add strip of fabric 1 to cover foundation.

Row 3

Row 2

Row 1

Fabric 2

14. Use the eight posies set aside when you were making the left front (see step 11 on page 39). Remove the backing paper and pin an appliqué to the center of each fabric 1 triangle on each sleeve. (If necessary for larger sizes, trace and cut additional posies.)

15. One by one, remove the pins from the appliqués and fuse in place. Follow the manufacturer's directions for fusing.

16. Using a contrasting-color thread and your favorite machine appliqué stitch, stitch around the outer edges of each appliqué.

17. Press the completed sleeve. Sew a button to the center of each posy.

WINNING TIP

Use a dab of glue stick to hold the buttons in position and stitch in place by machine. Adjust the zigzag stitch for the width of the holes and lower the feed dogs. If you have one for your machine, attach a button foot. Tie off the threads on the underside of the sleeves.

18. Machine baste contrasting piping to the outer-front jacket edges and the bottom edge of each sleeve. Use your adjusted zipper foot or a piping foot so that you can stitch as close as possible to the piping cord for a snug finish.

FINISHING THE JACKET

1. Cut two 3½"-wide strips of fabric 1 for the neckband.

2. Cut the jacket fronts, back, and sleeves from the lining fabric.

3. Refer to "Assembling the Jacket" on page 26 and "Finishing the Jacket" on page 28 to complete "Garden Melody."

4. Wear your new jacket with pride and go to your favorite fabric store to choose the fabrics for your next jazzy jacket or vest.

Fantasia

Front and Back Views

SHOPPING LIST

All yardage requirements listed are based on 44"-wide fabrics. You can use fat quarters for any fabric that requires ¼ yard if you prepare it for cutting as directed on page 10.

Basics

Jacket pattern: Pattern tracing paper or tissue paper and pattern pullouts included with this book

Vest foundation: 2 yards of cotton flannel or muslin

Vest lining: 2 yards of cotton print or solid

Interfacing: ⅜ yard of lightweight fusible interfacing (knit or weft-insertion type)

Patchwork Fabrics

All 12 fabrics are used for the fan patchwork on the vest back. Choose a large-scale, multi-colored print for fabric 8, and then pick three or four colors from the print as your guide for selecting a group of fabric coordinates. Strive for a pleasing balance of color and contrast, using a mix of tone-on-tone and busier prints. You may also use a solid fabric in the mix.

The descriptions with each of the fabrics in the list below are representative of those used in the vest pictured on page 44. Refer to them as guidelines.

Fabric 1: ⅓ yard of tone-on-tone or small-scale print for back, right front, and left front

Fabric 2: ⅛ yard of solid or small-scale print for back, right front, and left front

Fabric 3: ¼ yard of tone-on-tone print for back

Fabric 4: ¼ yard of tone-on-tone or small-scale print for back, right front, and left front

Fabric 5: ⅔ yard of tone-on-tone print or solid for back, right front, left front, front band, and armhole bands

Fabric 6: ¼ yard of large-scale or tone-on-tone print for back and right front

Fabric 7: ¼ yard of solid or tone-on-tone print for back, right front, and left front

Fabric 8: 1 yard of large-scale, multicolored print for back, right front, and left front

Fabric 9: ¼ yard of medium-scale or tone-on-tone print for back, right front, and left front

Fabric 10: ¼ yard of medium-scale or tone-on-tone print for back and right front

Fabric 11: ¼ yard of tone-on-tone print or solid for back and right front

Fabric 12: ¼ yard of solid or tone-on-tone print for back, right front, and left front

Notions and Special Supplies

- Thread to match patchwork fabrics

- 7 yards of braid trim for embellishing

- Rotary-cutting equipment: mat, ruler, and cutter

- Marilyn Doheny's original 9°, 22½"-long Circle Wedge Ruler. The patchwork Fantasy Fan in this vest represents only the tip of the iceberg when it comes to the designs that you can create using this unique cutting guide.

CAUTION: There are a variety of wedge-shaped rulers available. If you decide not to purchase Marilyn Doheny's ruler, be sure the one you choose is 22½" long and 1" wide at the short end.

Construction at a Glance

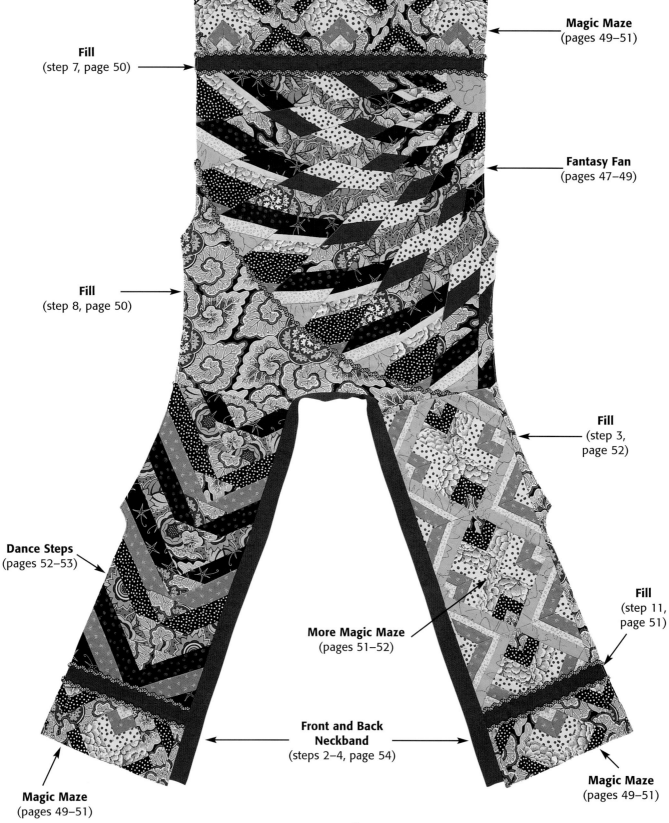

Magic Maze
(pages 49–51)

Fill
(step 7, page 50)

Fantasy Fan
(pages 47–49)

Fill
(step 8, page 50)

Fill
(step 3,
page 52)

Dance Steps
(pages 52–53)

Fill
(step 11,
page 51)

More Magic Maze
(pages 51–52)

**Front and Back
Neckband**
(steps 2–4, page 54)

Magic Maze
(pages 49–51)

Magic Maze
(pages 49–51)

GETTING READY TO SEW

1. On pattern tracing or tissue paper, trace the jacket front and back for your size from the pattern pullouts in this book. You will not use the sleeve pattern.

2. Use the jacket front and back pieces to cut the vest front and back pieces from the foundation fabric. Stay stitch the front and back neckline edges ⅜" from the raw edges.

3. Apply fusible interfacing to the wrong side of the foundation front and back (see illustration on page 15).

IMPORTANT NOTES

For all patchwork, cut all strips across the fabric width (selvage to selvage). If you are using fat quarters when the fabric requires ¼ yard, see the cutting and sewing illustration on page 10.

All patchwork seam allowances are ¼" wide. All garment construction seam allowances are ½" wide.

VEST BACK: FANTASY FAN

1. Following the chart, cut 1 strip of each fabric in the strip width indicated.

Fabrics	Strip Width
1 and 6	3"
2	1"
3 and 8	2½"
4, 5, 10, and 11	2"
7, 9, and 12	1½"

2. Arrange the strips in an order that creates good contrast from strip to strip. *Note that for strips in positions six or seven, it is very important to choose a fabric that provides a sharp contrast with the ones on either side of it. This fabric will be in the approximate center of the completed fan.* (See illustration in step 4 below.)

3. At the left end of each strip, fold the short end down to meet the long edge (45° angle) and crease. Then open the corner.

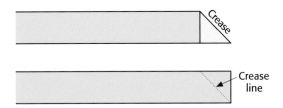

4. Sew the strips together in the order you've chosen, staggering the ends by placing the short end of the next strip at the crease in the previous one. Press the seams in one direction.

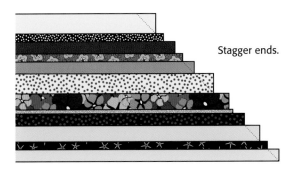

Stagger ends.

5. Using the 9° Circle Wedge Ruler as shown in the illustration on page 48, cut as many wedges as possible from the strip-pieced unit. Position the 45° line on the ruler parallel to a seam line on the strip unit. For each new cut, flip the ruler end to end in order to make opposite-angle cuts. The line will hit a different line of the patchwork when the large end of the ruler

is at the top of the fabric than it does when the small end is at the top of the fabric. This creates two different sets of wedges.

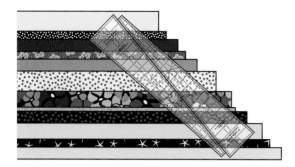

WINNING TIP

If the 45° line cannot be positioned exactly along or parallel to a seam line, it may be necessary to trim a sliver from the cut edge of the strip unit to re-angle the edge correctly so that it will. *It is essential to position the ruler correctly for each cut.*

6. Alternate the two different patchwork wedges. Sew them together to create the fan. Since the wedges are so long, it is helpful to pin them together at the beginning and end of the seam before stitching. (There are no seams to match.) Press all seams in one direction.

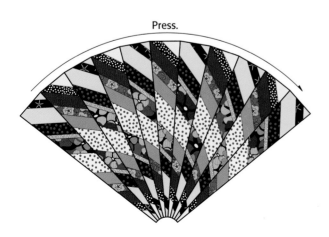

Press.

7. With the foundation face up on a flat surface, pin the fan in place with the lower-left edge along the side seam edge and up to the left shoulder. Make sure the lower edge of the fan is parallel and equidistant from the lower edge of the foundation. Some foundation will show at the left armhole edge. Trim the excess fan even with the foundation edges.

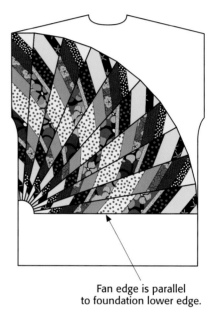

Fan edge is parallel
to foundation lower edge.

8. Use fan leftovers to cover any exposed foundation at the left armhole edge. Don't worry about trying to match the color positioning in the fan as this strip will be covered by the armhole band. With right sides together and raw edges even, stitch the strip to the edge and then flip it onto the foundation. Press and pin it in place. Trim it even with the foundation.

9. Make a template for the fan point by tracing the pattern on pullout 2B. Use the template to cut a piece from one of the 12 fabrics to cover the foundation at the end of the fan. Turn under and press ¼" along

the curved edge. Position it over the fan raw edge and machine or hand appliqué it in place. Trim it even with the foundation if necessary.

Appliqué in place.

10. Make and position the patchwork Magic Maze (see below) and then finish the vest back (page 50).

VEST HEM EDGES FOR RIGHT FRONT, LEFT FRONT, AND BACK: MAGIC MAZE

1. From each of fabrics 1, 2, 4, and 7, cut two 1½"-wide strips. From each of fabrics 8 and 12, cut two 2"-wide strips. From fabric 9, cut two 1"-wide strips.

2. Arrange seven strips (each a different fabric) in the desired order. Strips 1 and 7 will be the most prominent in this piece; use a stronger color or print in these positions so that they will pop and make the zigzag effect (see vest photos on page 44). Sew the strips together using ¼"-wide seams. The resulting strip unit should

measure 8" wide. Repeat with the remaining seven strips. Cut each strip unit into five 8" squares, for a total of ten squares. (Measure the strip units before cutting. If they are not both 8" wide, use the width of the narrowest strip unit to cut the squares.)

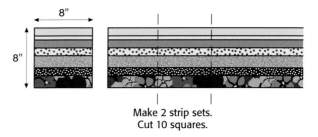

Make 2 strip sets.
Cut 10 squares.

3. Cut each square twice diagonally to yield a total of 40 triangles (A, B, C, D).

4. Following the illustrations below, arrange the triangles in two sets of 20 triangles.

Pattern 1

Pattern 2

5. Taking care to keep the triangles in the correct position, sew them together to create squares. Press the seams toward one of the triangles in each square. Sew the squares together to complete each row of 10 blocks. Press the seams in one direction.

6. Audition the two completed rows of Magic Maze to decide which one you like best at the lower edge of the vest back. Find the center seam by folding the chosen strip in half. Position it on the vest back foundation, with the lower edges even and the center seam at the center back. Pin it in place. Trim the excess patchwork even with the foundation at the side seam edges. You should have two equal lengths of Magic Maze for the vest fronts. Set these aside.

Sew trim over raw edges. →

Fabric 5

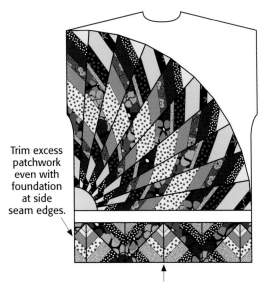

← Trim excess patchwork even with foundation at side seam edges.

Position seam at center back.

7. Measure the width of the exposed foundation between Fantasy Fan and Magic Maze. Cut a strip of fabric 5 this width plus ¾". With right sides together and raw edges even, stitch the strip to the upper edge of Magic Maze. Flip it onto the foundation and press. Tuck the upper edge under the lower edge of Fantasy Fan and pin. Trim the excess strip even with the foundation side seam edges. Zigzag stitch the raw edge in place. Cover the raw edge with decorative braid trim. Repeat at the seam line. Stitch. Refer to the illustration above right.

8. Cover the exposed foundation above the fan by tucking the raw edge of a piece of fabric 8 under the upper raw edge of the fan. Pin it in place. Trim the excess fabric even with the foundation. *Stitch in the ditch of every other long seam in the fan to anchor the fan to the foundation.* Zigzag stitch over the upper raw edge of the fan to hold the layers in place. Position decorative trim over the raw edges and stitch in place.

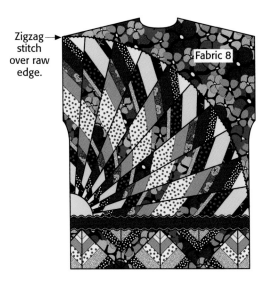

Zigzag stitch over raw edge. →

Fabric 8

9. Measure the width of the bottom edge of the vest right-front foundation and divide by two. Mark that measurement on the right-front foundation at the lower edge. From the mark, draw a straight line up to the shoulder. *Make sure the line is perpendicular to the lower edge of the foundation.* Repeat on the left-front foundation, ending the line about 8" above the bottom edge.

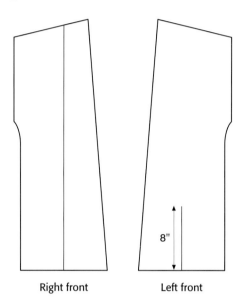

Right front   Left front

WINNING TIP

Make the marking easy and accurate by placing the bottom edge of the foundation along a horizontal line on your rotary-cutting mat. Follow a vertical line to draw a straight line to the shoulder.

10. At the lower edge of each vest-front foundation, position one of the Magic Maze pieces you set aside earlier. Match a vertical seam line with the line on the foundation. Pin in place. Cover any exposed foundation with a strip of fabric 8 using the stitch-and-flip method.

11. Cut a dividing strip from fabric 5 the same width as the one you added to the vest back. Stitch and flip the strip in place at the upper edge of each strip of Magic Maze on the fronts.

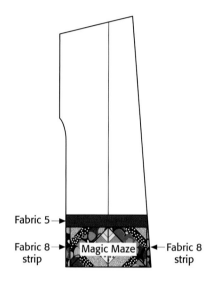

Fabric 5 →
Fabric 8 → strip   Magic Maze   ← Fabric 8 strip

LEFT FRONT: MORE MAGIC MAZE

1. Separate the remaining strip of Magic Maze blocks into two rows of five blocks each.

2. Position one of the strips on the left-front foundation. Make sure the lower edge is ⅛" below the upper edge of the dividing strip and the inner raw edge is ¼" past the marked line on the foundation. Arrange so that the left raw edge of the patchwork is even with the front raw edge of the foundation. A small amount of foundation will be exposed at the upper edge of the strip. Pin the patchwork in place.

51

NOTE: These blocks will form two different patterns, depending on which long side of the strips you sew together. Test both arrangements and choose the one you like best.

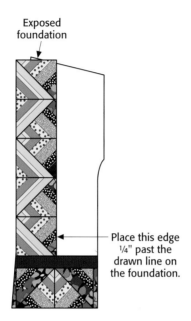

Exposed foundation

Place this edge ¼" past the drawn line on the foundation.

3. Stitch and flip the remaining strip of Magic Maze in place on the left front foundation. Cover the exposed foundation at the shoulder, side seam, and armhole edges with one of the more inconspicuous fabrics from your selection. Cut a strip wide enough to cover the area, and stitch and flip it in place. Press the completed work. Zigzag over the upper raw edge of the fabric 5 dividing strip. Cover the raw edges and the seam line with trim and stitch in place.

Cover exposed foundation.

RIGHT FRONT: DANCE STEPS

1. From fabric 8, cut seven 3⅞" squares. Cut the squares in half diagonally to make 14 triangles.

2. From each of fabrics 1, 6, 7, 10, and 11, cut one 2"-wide strip.

3. On the right-front foundation, draw a line 1" from the shoulder at the front edge. Make it perpendicular to the first line you drew on the foundation. This is the placement line for the long edge of the first triangle. With the point facing down and the long edge at the marked line, pin the first triangle in place.

4. To cover the foundation above the horizontal line, stitch and flip a strip of fabric (fabric 8 works best) to the long edge of the triangle.

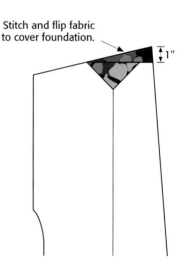

Stitch and flip fabric to cover foundation.

1"

5. With right sides together, stitch a 2"-wide strip of fabric from step 2 to the right edge of the triangle. Flip the strip onto the foundation, press, and pin in place. Trim the strip even with the foundation edges. Repeat on the opposite edge of the triangle, *using the same fabric and setting*

the lower end of the strip ¼" below the triangle point. Do not cover more than ¼" of the first strip with the second. Stitch and flip. Press and trim.

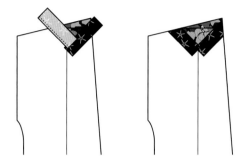

6. Mark the center of the long edge of the next triangle by folding and creasing it. With right sides together and the ¼" seam line of the second triangle at the point of the first triangle, pin and stitch the long edge of the triangle to the foundation. Trim any excess from the first two strips underneath the triangle edge even with the triangle raw edge.

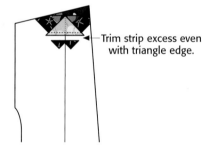

Trim strip excess even with triangle edge.

7. Flip the triangle down onto the foundation and press. The point of the triangle should be in line with the vertical line drawn on the foundation. Pin in place.

8. Choose another 2"-wide strip from step 2 and add a second set of strips as described in step 5.

9. Continue adding triangles and strips until you reach a point where no more triangles will fit completely on the foundation (the size Small vest requires 11 triangles). Add two more strips to the triangle, extending the second one so that it is hidden under the loose upper edge of the dividing strip cut from fabric 5.

10. Continue adding strips in pairs to cover the remaining exposed foundation, ending each one just under the dividing strip. Zigzag over the raw edge of the dividing strip. Cover the dividing-strip raw edge and the lower seam with trim to match the vest back. (See illustration with steps 9 and 10 on page 54.)

11. Stitch ⅛" from all raw edges.

FINISHING THE VEST

Vest seam allowances are ½" wide.

1. With right sides together and raw edges even, sew the patchwork fronts to the back at the shoulders and side seam edges. Press the seams open. Repeat with the lining pieces.

2. From fabric 5, cut two 3½"-wide strips for the front band (cutting across the fabric width).

3. From the fusible interfacing, cut two 3¼"-wide strips the length of the front-band strips. Center the interfacing on the wrong side of the band strips and fuse in place, following the manufacturer's directions.

4. Assemble the bands and sew to the vest front and back neckline edges as directed in steps 8–12 for "Jazz Squared" on page 27.

5. *With right sides together,* pin the lining to the patchwork vest, making sure the layers are smooth and wrinkle-free. Stitch ½" from the raw edges. Trim the seams to ¼", trim the corners, and clip the curves. Turn right side out through one of the armholes and press.

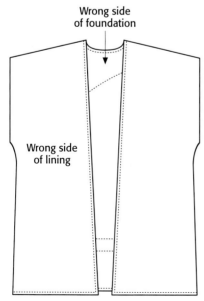

Sew lining to vest around back and front neckline and bottom edges.

6. Measure the vest armhole edge and add ½" for seams. From fabric 5, cut two 2½"-wide strips to this length for the armhole bands. Sew the short ends together using a ¼"-wide seam. Press the seam open.

7. With raw edges even *and the right side of the armhole band against the vest lining,* pin in place. Stitch ½" from the raw edges.

8. Press the strip toward the seam allowance. Bring the raw edge of the armhole band to meet the raw edge of the armhole seam and press. Turn the band to the patchwork side, encasing the armhole raw edge (the raw edge will be inside the band at the fold line). Press and pin in place.

9. Edgestitch in place through all layers. Finish the remaining armhole in the same manner.

10. Beginning close to the underarm seam, position braid trim on the patchwork vest. Center it over the edge of the band and turn under the end where it meets the beginning of the trim. Stitch in place. Embellish the seam line next to the bands on the front and back neckline in the same manner.

11. Wear your new vest with pride and start planning your next project!

Patched Rhythms

Front and Back Views

SHOPPING LIST

All yardage requirements listed are based on 44"-wide fabrics. You can use fat quarters for any fabric that requires ¼ yard if you prepare it for cutting as directed on page 10.

Basics

- Vest pattern: Pattern tracing paper or tissue paper and pattern pullouts included with this book

- Vest foundation: 1 to 1⅜ yards of cotton muslin or flannel

- Vest lining: 1 to 1⅜ yards of cotton print or solid

- Interfacing: ¾ yard of lightweight fusible interfacing (woven, knit, or weft-insertion type)

Patchwork Fabrics

- Choose fabrics in two distinct color families; for example, purple and yellow or orange and teal. Include some prints that are large scale and one that is tone on tone. Make sure there is value contrast between the two color families.

- Fabrics 1–10 are used for the patchwork vest fronts and back. Fabric 1 will be very noticeable on both vest fronts, so choose this fabric carefully.

Color Family A

Fabric 1: ½ yard tone-on-tone print for the bars and lattice on the vest fronts and the block centers for the vest back

Fabrics 6, 7, 8, and 9: ¼ yard each for patchwork

Color Family B

Fabrics 2, 3, 4, 5, and 10: ¼ yard each for patchwork

Notions and Special Supplies

- Thread to match the fabrics

- 30 to 35 buttons in assorted sizes for embellishing the patchwork fronts

- Rotary-cutting equipment (mat, ruler, and cutter)

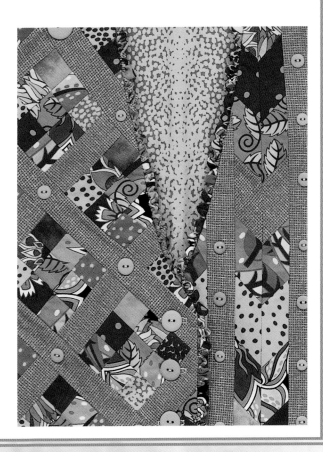

Construction at a Glance

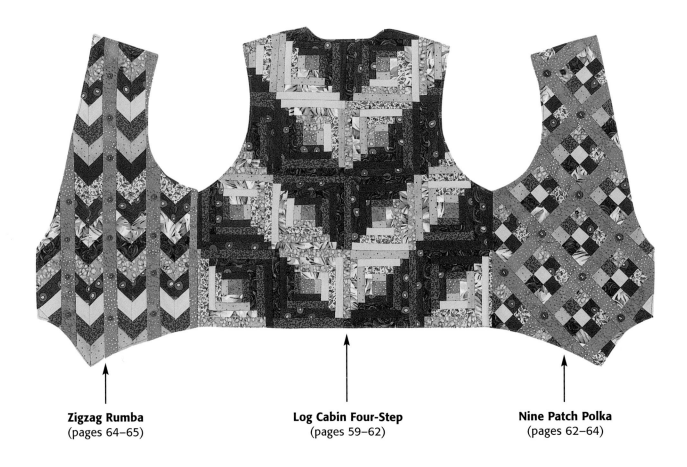

Zigzag Rumba
(pages 64–65)

Log Cabin Four-Step
(pages 59–62)

Nine Patch Polka
(pages 62–64)

GETTING READY TO SEW

1. On pattern tracing or tissue paper, trace the vest front and back for your size from the pattern pullouts in this book.

   Note: It is important to shorten the front and back pattern pieces as indicated because the yardage is given for the shorter vest version.

2. Cut the pieces from the lining and the foundation fabrics. Stay stitch the front and back neckline edges of the lining ⅜" from the raw edges to prevent stretching. Set the lining pieces aside. Stay stitch the back neckline edge of the foundation ⅜" from the raw edge.

3. Cut 2"-wide strips of fusible interfacing for the center front and bottom edges and use the pattern as a guide. For the vest back, cut a 2½"-wide strip the length of the lower edge.

4. Fuse the interfacing to the wrong side of the vest foundation pieces.

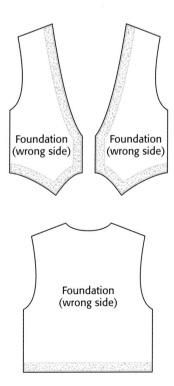

Foundation
(wrong side)   Foundation
(wrong side)

Foundation
(wrong side)

BACK: LOG CABIN FOUR-STEP

1. From fabric 1 (color family A), cut six strips, each 1½" wide. You will use these strips for the Log Cabin block centers, the left-front patchwork, and the sashing strips on both fronts. Set five strips aside for the fronts. From the remaining strip, cut 16 squares, each 1½" x 1½", for sizes Petite through Medium. Cut 20 squares for the remaining two larger sizes. These squares will be used for the Log Cabin block centers.

2. From each of the remaining nine fabrics, cut four 1"-wide strips. Group the strips in color family A and color family B.

3. Make 16 (for the three smaller sizes) or 20 (for the two larger sizes) Log Cabin blocks using the chain-piecing method that follows. You will add two color family A strips to a center square, followed by two color family B strips to complete each of the four rounds of logs required for each block.

   With right sides facing, pin a center square face down at one end of a color family A strip. Stitch ¼" from the raw edges. Before you reach the bottom edge of the square, add another square to the strip. *Make sure the square raw edges are even with the long edge of the strip and the upper edge of the square is just below (but not overlapping) the lower edge of the first square.* The raw edges of the two squares should just touch. Continue stitching, adding new squares until they are all attached to the strip. Cut the strip between the squares. Press the seam away from the center square in each of the units.

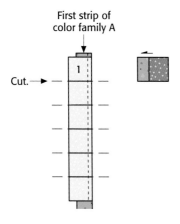

First strip of
color family A

Cut. →

1

WINNING TIP

Make the pressing faster and easier by following this tip. Place all units on the ironing surface, with the color family A strip on top. Use the point of the iron to press the strip away from the center square. You will develop a pressing rhythm. *Don't be tempted to press before cutting the units apart.* It's easier to press them after they are separated.

4. Place the pressed units face down on a different strip of fabric from color family A, with the first strip of color family A at the top and perpendicular to the long edge of the new strip. In other words, *the last strip added will be the first fabric under the needle when sewing the units to the new strip.* (That's my mantra as I chain piece Log Cabin blocks.) Stitch, clip apart, and press the units as directed in the previous step.

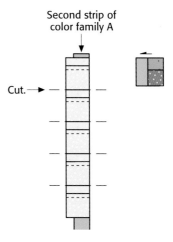

Second strip of
color family A

Cut. →

5. Choose a strip of color family B for the third round. Position each new unit on the strip as shown and stitch. Cut apart and press.

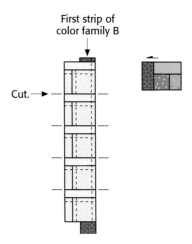

First strip of
color family B

Cut. →

6. Choose a different strip of color family B for the fourth round. Stitch each unit to the strip. Cut apart and press.

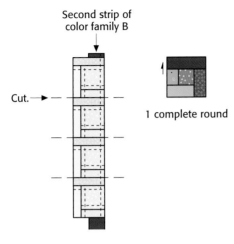

Second strip of color family B

Cut. ➔

1 complete round

7. Repeat the above steps to add three more rounds to each block. Begin each round with two strips of color family A, followed by two strips of color family B.

Make 16 for P, S, and M sizes.
Make 20 for L and XL sizes.

WINNING TIP

After you add four strips to the block center, it's easy to determine which edge should be stitched to the next strip. Look for the only strip on the block that has a seam line across *both* ends. Identify its color family and sew it to a strip from the same color family.

Seam   Seam

Rotate so you can stitch this edge to the next strip.

8. The blocks should measure 5½" square. If necessary, trim them all to a uniform size. Make sure, however, to trim as little as possible.

9. On the right side of the back foundation and beginning at the bottom edge, arrange the blocks in horizontal rows. Follow the shaded illustration below and rotate the blocks as needed so that the color families are in the correct location. (The blocks will extend past the foundation edges. Do not trim until directed to do so.)

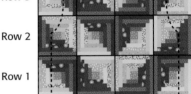

Row 4

Row 3

Row 2

Row 1

10. Remove the blocks from the foundation, keeping them in the correct order. Fold the foundation in half lengthwise with raw edges even and press to mark the center back.

11. Sew the blocks for row 1 together and press the seams in one direction. Center the completed row on the foundation, right side up and lower raw edges even. If the row is not long enough to cover the foundation from edge to edge, add strips of the last color family at the short edges. Pin the row in place and trim any excess fabric even with the foundation side seam edges.

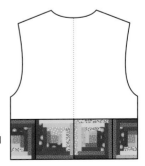

Row 1

12. Sew the blocks for row 2 together and press the seams in the opposite direction from row 1. Place row 2 face down on row 1. Make sure the bottom edge of row 2 is even with the upper edge of row 1 and that the seam lines match. If the row is not long enough to cover the foundation, add strips of the last color family at the short edges. Stitch ¼" from the raw edges. Flip the row up onto the foundation and press. Pin and trim even with the foundation as needed.

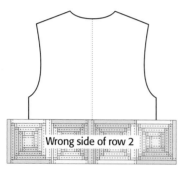

Place row 2 on top of row 1,
right sides together. Stitch.

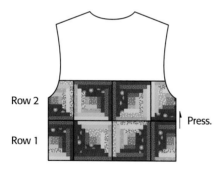

13. Sew the remaining rows together and add them to the foundation in the same manner as row 2. If the foundation still shows at the shoulders, use block cutaways or strip leftovers to cover the exposed areas. Stitch and flip in place. Press and trim. Stitch ⅛" from all raw edges.

RIGHT FRONT: NINE PATCH POLKA

1. Cut a 1½"-wide strip from each of fabrics 2 through 10. Cut each strip in half so that the strips measure approximately 22" long. Set aside one strip from each color for use later in "Rose-Petal Edging" on page 66.

2. Sew the remaining nine strips together in sets of three, using three different fabrics in each of the three strip units. Press the seams in one direction.

3. From each strip unit, cut 16 segments, each 1½" wide, for a total of 48 segments.

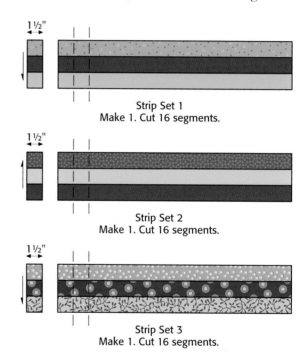

Strip Set 1
Make 1. Cut 16 segments.

Strip Set 2
Make 1. Cut 16 segments.

Strip Set 3
Make 1. Cut 16 segments.

4. Arrange the segments into a total of 16 blocks, using three different segments in each block. Each of the nine fabrics you used should appear only once in each block. Join the segments, matching seam

lines. Make a total of 16 Nine Patch blocks, each 3½" square. Press the seams in one direction.

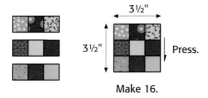

Make 16.

5. From the remaining 1½"-wide strips of fabric 1 (cut when you made the Log Cabin blocks for the vest back), cut 12 sashing strips, each 3½" long. Sew a strip to one edge of each of 12 Nine Patch blocks. Press the seam allowance toward the sashing in each unit.

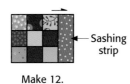

← Sashing strip

Make 12.

6. With the ruler at the underarm corner of the right-front foundation, position the 45° line parallel to the vest side seam. Draw a placement line from the underarm to the lower front edge.

Align 45° line along side seam edge.

Draw placement line.

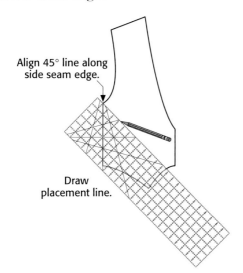

7. Position a 1½"-wide strip of fabric 1 *above the line,* with the lower raw edge at the line. Trim the strip even with the foundation.

8. Arrange a row of Nine Patch blocks above the strip. Make sure each short sashing strip is to the right of the Nine Patch. (Do not stitch yet.) Overlap the blocks ½" to allow for seams so that you are sure you have enough to cover the foundation once the blocks are sewn to the foundation.

9. Sew the blocks together in order and press the seams toward the short sashing strips. Place the completed patchwork strip face down, with the lower edge of the blocks even with the upper edge of the 1½"-wide sashing. Pin the strip in place. Stitch ¼" from the raw edges. Flip the patchwork strip onto the foundation and press. Pin it in place and trim the strip even with the foundation.

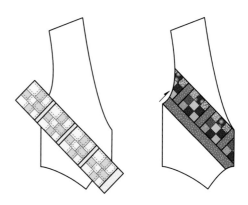

10. In the same manner, stitch another long sashing strip to the upper edge of the row of blocks. Trim the strip even with the foundation. To accurately align the short sashing strips from row to row, place a ruler along the short sashing seam lines and make marks on the foundation beyond each long sashing strip.

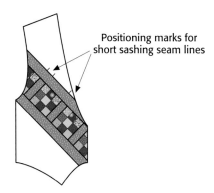

Positioning marks for short sashing seam lines

11. Arrange, stitch, and flip additional rows of patchwork and sashing to cover the foundation all the way to the upper and lower edges. Press. Stitch ⅛" from all raw edges.

12. Sew a button to the sashing at each intersection.

LEFT FRONT: ZIGZAG RUMBA

1. Position the left-front foundation face up on a lined cutting mat. Make sure the front edge is along a line. Measure and draw a line parallel to the center front edge that intersects the lower front point. Draw a second line *¼" to the right of the first drawn line*. This second line is the placement line for the raw edge of the first piece of zigzag patchwork. Set the foundation aside.

← →¼"

2. From each of the 10 fabrics, cut one 1½"-wide strip for a total of 10 strips. For a different result, you may choose not to use fabric 1. Instead, cut a second strip from one of the other 9 fabrics. Compare the left front in the photo on page 58 with the left front on page 56. Use the remaining sashing strips (cut when you made the Log Cabin blocks for the vest back) for the bars of color between the 10 strips.

3. Alternating the 10 strips by color and contrast, sew them together to create a strip unit that will measure 10½" wide. Press the seams in one direction.

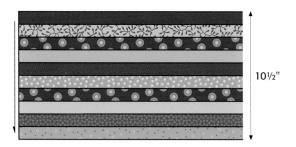

10½"

4. Fold the strip unit in half crosswise *with wrong sides together and seam lines aligned*. Place the 45° line of a long rotary ruler parallel to one of the seam lines and close to the folded edge. Cutting at a 45° angle, make a total of seven cuts spaced 1½" apart for a total of 12 strips. The seams will angle in opposite directions in

each cut set. As needed, cut strips apart along the fold to separate them. Some sets will be longer than others. Set aside the cutaway pieces of the strip unit in case you need to cut more strips for additional length.

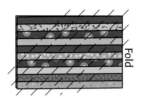

Cut strips at 45° angle.

Cut strips apart at fold.

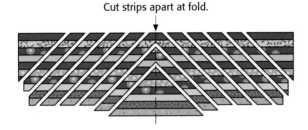

5. Arrange the strips in matching pairs on your work surface to create the zigzag pattern shown.

Arrange in zigzag pairs.

6. Position one of the two strips in the longest set of zigzag patchwork on the left-front foundation to the right of the placement line. Make sure the strip right side is facing up and the raw edge is at the placement line. If either strip is not long enough to cover the foundation from top to bottom, cut another strip from the leftovers and sew to one end, making sure that the fabric positions repeat in the same order. Pin the strip in place. Pin the second strip on top of the first strip, with right sides together, raw edges even, and seam intersections matching. Stitch ¼" from the raw edges through the foundation. Flip the top strip onto the foundation and press. Pin in place. Trim the strips even with the foundation edges.

7. Stitch and flip 1½"-wide fabric 1 sashing strips to the right and left edges of the zigzag patchwork. Press and pin in place. Trim even with the foundation.

8. In the same manner, add a set of zigzag patchwork to the *left* of the first set of strips and sashing, taking care to match the patchwork point positions across the front.

9. Cover the remainder of the foundation to the right of the first set of strips with zigzag patchwork and sashing strips. Press and trim even with the foundation. Stitch ⅛" from the raw edges. Save any leftover strips for "Rose-Petal Edging." Arrange buttons as desired along the sashing strips and sew in place.

ROSE-PETAL EDGING

Vest seam allowances are ½" wide.

1. With right sides together and raw edges even, sew the patchwork fronts to the back at the shoulders and side seam edges. Press the seams open. Repeat with the lining pieces.

2. Measure the distance around the outer edge of the vest. Using diagonal seams, sew leftover 1½"-wide strips from all of the patchwork to make a scrappy strip twice the distance measurement for "Rose-Petal Edging." If the strips are longer than 12", cut them into shorter pieces before sewing them together. Press the seams open.

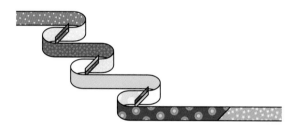

3. Sew the short ends of the strip together to make a circle. Press the seam open. Fold the pieced strip in half lengthwise with *wrong sides together* and raw edges even. Press. Machine baste ¼" from the raw edges. Draw up the stitching to gather the strip and make a ruffle that will fit around the vest outer edge.

WINNING TIP

If you have a gathering foot, use it to eliminate the necessity of drawing up the stitching and adjusting the gathers in the rose-petal strip. Many machines will automatically gather the fabric if you increase the tension and stitch length. Test it on scraps to see if it works for you.

4. Pin and machine baste the ruffle to the right side of the vest ¼" from the raw edges (neckline, front, and lower edges).

5. *With right sides together* and raw edges even, pin and stitch the lining to the vest all the way around the outside edge (but not the armholes). Use a ¼"-wide seam allowance. Clip the points and curves. Turn the vest right side out through one of the open armholes. Press along the outer edges of the vest. Take care not to flatten the ruffle.

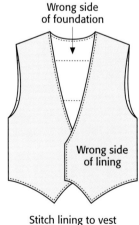

Wrong side
of foundation

Wrong side
of lining

Stitch lining to vest
around outside edge.

6. Thread a needle with a double thread and knot. Insert the needle in the lining at the lower edge of the vest and bring the thread to the right side at the base of the ruffle; pop the knot through the lining so that it is between the foundation and the lining. Stitch over the ruffle two or three times, pulling the thread tight with each stitch. Bring the thread to the lining side and slip the needle between the foundation and the lining, coming to the front ½" from the previous stitching. Stitch over the ruffle two or three times as before. Con-tinue all the way around the vest.

7. Measure the vest armhole edge. Add ½" to the distance around the vest armhole edge. Sew enough leftover 1½"-wide strips together to make a binding strip of this length. Make a second strip of the same length. Sew the short ends together in each strip to make a circle for each armhole. Fold each circular strip in half lengthwise *with wrong sides together* and raw edges even. Press.

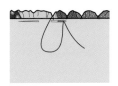

8. Pin a binding strip to each armhole edge *on the lining side,* beginning near the side seam.

9. Stitch the binding in place using a ¼"-wide seam allowance. Turn the binding to the right side of the vest and pin in place. Use a long straight stitch or a decorative machine stitch to topstitch the folded edge in place.

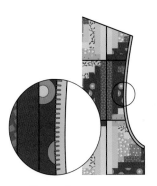

Decorative
blanket stitch

Dancing in the Cabin

Front and Back Views

Construction at a Glance

Fill
(step 13,
page 77)

Wacky Logs
(pages
76–77)

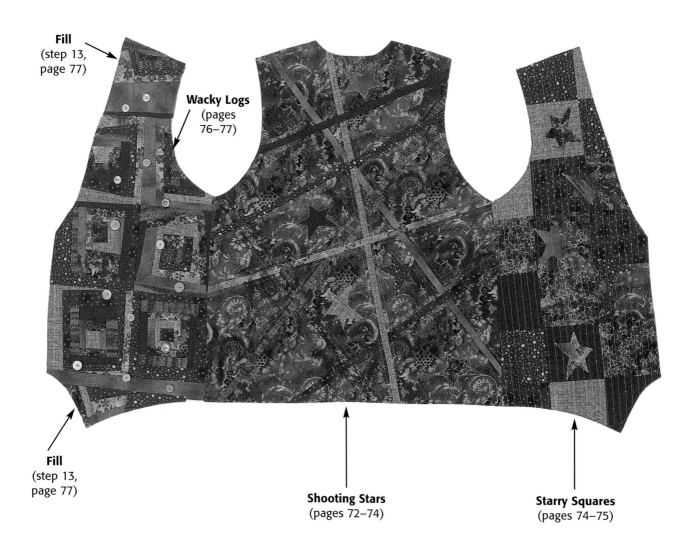

Fill
(step 13,
page 77)

Shooting Stars
(pages 72–74)

Starry Squares
(pages 74–75)

SHOPPING LIST

All yardage requirements listed are based on 44"-wide fabrics. You can use fat quarters for any fabric that requires ¼ yard if you prepare it for cutting as directed on page 10.

Basics

- **Vest pattern:** Pattern tracing paper or tissue paper and pattern sheets included with this book

- **Vest foundation:** 1 to 1⅜ yards of cotton muslin or flannel

- **Vest lining:** 1 to 1⅜ yards of cotton print or solid

- **Interfacing:** ⅜ yard of lightweight fusible interfacing (woven, knit, or weft-insertion type)

Patchwork Fabrics

Choose a bright print or tone-on-tone print with lots of colors for the vest back and then choose the remaining fabrics to coordinate with it. Remember that this fabric will be the backdrop for the shooting star appliqués. It will also be included in the patchwork for the vest fronts.

Fabric 1: 1 yard for vest back and front patch-work

Fabrics 2, 3, 4, 5, 6: ¼ yard each for patchwork and stars

Fabric 7: ½ yard for patchwork, stars, and outer bias

Fabric 8: ½ yard for patchwork and stars

Fabric 9: ½ yard for patchwork, stars, and inner bias

Notions and Special Supplies

Thread to match the fabrics

- Decorative thread for embellishment, such as variegated rayon or metallic threads

- Beading thread (Nymo or Silamide)

- Paper-backed fusible web for star appliqués

- 15–25 assorted small to medium buttons, including 4 for the front-button closure

- Small seed beads for shimmer

- Rotary-cutting equipment (mat, ruler, and cutter)

- Optional: Sharp, pointed scissors (for slashing stars on vest front), walking foot, and ½" bias tape maker

GETTING READY TO SEW

1. On pattern tracing or tissue paper, trace the vest front and back for your size from the pattern sheets in this book.

2. Cut the pieces from the lining and the foundation fabrics. Stay stitch the front and back neckline edges of the lining ⅜" from the raw edges to prevent stretching. Set the lining pieces aside. Stay stitch the back neckline edge of the foundation.

3. Using the pattern as a guide, cut 2"-wide fusible interfacing for the center front and bottom edges. For the vest back, cut a 2½"-wide strip the length of the lower edge.

4. Fuse the interfacing to the wrong side of the vest foundation pieces (see illustrations on page 59).

IMPORTANT NOTES

For all patchwork, cut all strips across the fabric width (selvage to selvage). If you are using fat quarters when the fabric requires ¼ yard, see the cutting and sewing illustration on page 10.

All patchwork seam allowances are ¼" wide. All garment construction seam allowances are ½" wide.

BACK: SHOOTING STARS

1. Position the vest back foundation on top of fabric 1 and use it as a guide to cut a vest back, *cutting it ¼" larger all around.* Set the foundation piece aside.

2. From each of the remaining fabrics, cut one strip, 1" x 42", for a total of eight strips.

3. Position one strip from step 2 on the back, right side up and at an angle. It should go from edge to edge and in the direction of your choice. *Do not trim the strip yet.*

4. When you are happy with the strip position, place your rotary ruler on top of the strip, with the ½" ruler line along one edge. *Leaving the ruler in place, carefully remove the strip.* Cut along the ruler edge to divide the back into two pieces.

5. With right sides together and at least ½" of the strip extending past both edges, stitch the strip to the larger of the two back pieces. Make sure you are stitching an accurate ¼"-wide seam. Press the seam toward the strip and trim the excess even with the vest-back edges.

6. With the vest-back pieces face up on your work surface, align the remaining vest and strip raw edges so that when you sew the pieces together, the vest will be the original shape. Pin with right sides together

and stitch an accurate ¼" seam, stitching from the strip side. If you are using a ¼" patchwork foot, the edge should just touch the raw edge of the first seam. Working from the right side, press the seam toward the strip. *Don't worry; adding the strip this way will not make the vest smaller.*

7. With the vest back facing up, add another strip, crossing the first at an angle and extending from one vest edge to another. Follow steps 4–6 to cut the vest apart and add the strip. Pin carefully so that the second half of the vest matches the new strip and the vest shape remains intact.

8. Continue in the same fashion to add a total of eight strips that crisscross the back.

9. Place the pieced vest back right side up on top of the slightly smaller back foundation. Pin it in place. *Do not trim yet.*

10. Using a slightly longer stitch than normal and a decorative thread on top, machine stitch ¼" away from each side of each strip. Begin with the center-most strip and work outward from there. Stop stitching wherever one strip crosses under another and tie off the threads on the wrong side. Begin stitching again on the other side of the strip underneath.

WINNING TIP

To continuously stitch along the edge of a strip *without* stitching across the strip underneath, lock the stitches at the edge of a crossing strip by shortening the stitch as you approach the crossing strip. Then set your machine at zero stitch length and stitch in place. Next, raise the needle and presser foot and reposition the fabric so that you can lower the needle in the fabric on the other side of the strip. Begin by stitching in place. Then lengthen the stitch and continue stitching until you reach the end or the next strip intersection. Continue in this fashion until you stitch all the strip edges in place. Pull the knots to the back side. Clip the floating threads on top.

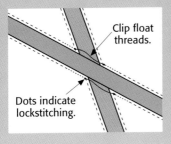

Clip float threads.

Dots indicate lockstitching.

11. Trace 9 to 12 stars (pattern pullout 2B) onto the paper side of the fusible web, leaving about ½" of space between each star. Cut out the stars, leaving a ¼" margin around each one.

12. Fuse the stars to the wrong side of small pieces of any of fabrics 2–9 that contrast with fabric 1.

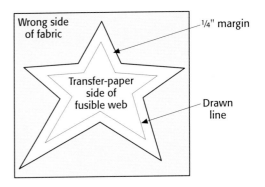

Wrong side of fabric

¼" margin

Transfer-paper side of fusible web

Drawn line

13. Cut out the stars on the drawn lines. Use a pin to anchor each of several stars to the vest back. Try to use an uneven number. You may place stars in open areas between crossed strips as well as on top of strips. When you are pleased with the arrangement, remove the pin from a star and fuse it in place, following the manufacturer's directions. Continue until all the star appliqués are fused. Save any remaining stars for the right front.

14. Embellish and anchor the outer edges of the stars with your favorite machine appliqué stitch.

WINNING TIP

At the points and corners of the star appliqués, stop with the needle down in the fabric to the right of the appliqué edge. Raise the foot and pivot as needed so that you can continue stitching without the stitches piling up in one place.

15. For added sparkle, consider arranging a scattering of seed beads along the stitching lines that outline the strips and stars. Sew the beads in place by hand.

16. Trim the excess fabric 1 even with the outer edges of the vest back foundation as needed. Stitch ⅛" from the outer edges.

RIGHT FRONT: STARRY SQUARES

1. On the right side of both left- and right-front foundations, draw a patchwork placement line across the widest point. Set the left-front foundation aside.

2. Measure the drawn line and divide by three for the size of the finished squares you will sew to the front. *Add ½" to this measurement* for seam allowances.

Draw line and measure.
Divide by 3. Add ½".

3. Using the size determined in step 2, cut three squares from each of fabrics 1, 3, 4, 5, 6, and 7 (a total of 18 squares).

4. Place the foundation face up on a flat surface. Beginning at the drawn line, place squares on the foundation until it is completely covered above the line. Overlap squares by about ½" to allow for seams. When you are pleased with the arrangement of the squares, move the rows to one side and keep the squares in order.

5. Sew the squares for row 1 together and press the seams in one direction. Center the completed row right side up on the foundation. Make sure the bottom edge of the row is along the drawn line. Pin the row in place and trim it even with the foundation if necessary.

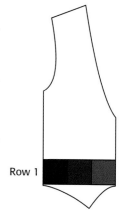

Row 1

6. Sew the squares for row 2 together and press the seams in the opposite direction from row 1. With right sides together and seam lines matching, align the bottom edge of row 2 with the upper edge of row 1. Stitch ¼" from the raw edges. Flip the strip onto the foundation. Press and pin it in place.

7. Assemble the remaining rows and sew them to the foundation in the same manner as row 2. You won't need all three blocks in the upper areas of the vest. Use a scrap in place of the square in those areas if you wish. Trim excess fabric even with the foundation. Stitch ⅛" from the raw edges.

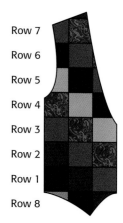

Row 7
Row 6
Row 5
Row 4
Row 3
Row 2
Row 1
Row 8

8. Fuse the stars remaining from the vest back (see steps 11–13 of "Back: Shooting Stars" on page 73), to the wrong side of matching fabric to make double-sided stars. Cut out each star.

9. Scatter the stars across the vest-front patchwork and arrange as desired (refer to vest photos on pages 69–70). Prepare more stars if needed. Pin stars in place.

10. Beginning at the center of the shoulder edge of the vest front and using decorative thread in the needle, stitch through all the fabric layers to the bottom edge. Continue to sew in this manner to cover the vest front with rows of stitching spaced ½" apart.

WINNING TIP

If you use a walking foot for the stitching, use the width of the foot as your measuring gauge for the rows.

11. Optional: Slip the point of your scissors under the edge of a star between the stitching lines and slash. Repeat between all lines of stitching on each star. This step adds unexpected texture.

12. With a fine hand-sewing needle and knotted double beading thread (Nymo or Silamide), add four seed beads to each star point. Bring the thread up from the wrong side of the vest front and out about ¼" in from a star point. Put four beads on the needle and slip them down the thread to the fabric. Holding the beads in place with a little slack in the thread, pass the needle down into the vest close to the last bead. Bring the needle up to the right side again. Pass the needle through the beads and back into the fabric. Take several small stitches in one place on the foundation side to secure the beads. Bead every point of every star in this manner. This step is essential if you slashed the stars because the beading keeps any loose points in place on the vest surface.

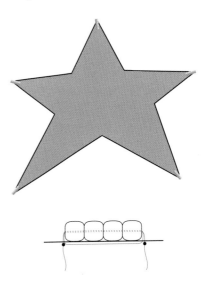

13. Stitch seed beads in place along the stitched lines as desired to add a little sparkle.

Slash star only,
between rows of stitching.

75

LEFT FRONT: WACKY LOGS

1. Measure the line you drew on the left-front vest foundation (see step 1 of "Right Front: Starry Squares" on page 74) and divide by two. Add ½". Following the directions below, make six blocks this size. (For size Small, the measurement is 6½".)

2. Divide your fabrics into four color families; for example, turquoise, black, pink, and orange. You may have one or more fabrics in each group.

3. Cut a square or rectangle for the center of each block. For a playful look, don't make the centers all the same size or the same fabric. Mix it up! These center pieces should measure no larger than 2½" x 3".

4. From each color-family group, cut a variety of strips that vary in width from ¾" to 2" wide. For best results, do not strive to cut these strips in totally accurate widths. Allow the ruler to slip a bit so that some strips are more angular than others. Refer to the vest photo for an idea of how "wacky" the strips can be.

5. Choose a strip from one of the color families and sew a center square or rectangle from a different color family to the strip. Trim the strip edges even with the center piece. Flip the strip away from the center and press.

6. Working clockwise around the center, continue to add strips from the same color family (not necessarily the same fabric) until you complete a round with four strips.

7. Add a round of strips from each of the three remaining color families in the same manner (four rounds total). Make the block a bit larger than the required block size you determined earlier. You may need to play catch-up on the last round by sewing on wider strips so that the lopsided block is large enough for you to trim to size (see step 1).

 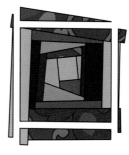

Lopsided Block.   Trim.

8. Begin the next block with a center piece of a different color and alter the color placement in the rounds so that your resulting blocks are different. Make a total of six blocks in this manner and trim them to the size determined in step 1.

9. Beginning at the drawn line on the left-front foundation, arrange the completed and trimmed blocks in three rows. Using a ¼" seam allowance, sew the blocks together in rows and press the seams in opposite directions from row to row.

10. Position row 1 on the foundation. Make sure the bottom edge of the row is along the drawn line; pin it in place. Trim any excess even with the foundation.

11. With right sides together and seam lines matching, add row 2 to the upper edge of row 1. Stitch and flip row 2 into position on the foundation. Press, pin, and trim the excess even with the foundation edges.

12. Add the third row in the same manner as row 2.

13. Cover the remainder of the foundation above and below the blocks with strips of random-width strips cut from your vest fabrics or cutaways from Wacky Logs. Stitch and flip the strips in place, one by one, and trim them even with the foundation. Machine stitch ⅛" from all raw edges.

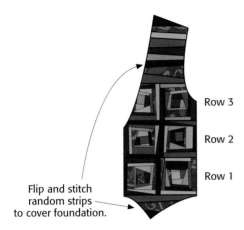

Row 3
Row 2
Row 1

Flip and stitch random strips to cover foundation.

14. With the completed left front face up on your work surface, toss a handful of buttons over the surface. Rearrange as desired. Mark the position of each one with a pin. Sew the buttons in place using a doubled thread. If you want to bead the buttons (see step 15), use beading thread in the needle.

15. Optional: After anchoring a button with a few stitches, bring the needle up through a hole and slide on a few seed beads. If the holes in the button are large, the beads may slip into the hole; that's okay. Continue adding beads until they reach the other hole. Take the needle through the hole to the back and bring it back up through the beads and button before securing the thread on the wrong side.

Beaded Button

TWO-STEP BIAS FINISH

Vest seam allowances are ½"-wide.

1. With right sides together and raw edges even, sew the patchwork fronts to the back at the shoulders and side seam edges. Press the seams open. Repeat with the lining pieces.

2. *With wrong sides together,* pin the lining to the patchwork vest. Make sure the layers are smooth and wrinkle free before machine basting them together ⅜" from the raw edges.

3. From fabric 7, cut 1¼"-wide true bias strips for the bias strips on the outer edges. From fabric 9, cut 1"-wide true bias strips for the inner bias strips. You will need enough strips of each fabric to total approximately five yards. Sew each set of strips together using bias seams and press the seams open to make two long strips.

4. At one short end of the 1¼"-wide strip, turn under and press ¼".

5. Beginning with the pressed end at a side seam at the vest lower edge, machine stitch the 1¼"-wide bias strip to the vest on the lining side. Use a ¼"-wide seam allowance. Keep the raw edges even and continue around the outer edges of the vest, mitering the bias strip at the front points. Lap the bias strip over the pressed end at the side seam and trim away the excess bias strip.

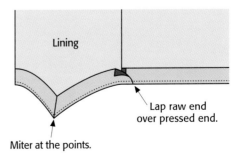

Lining

Lap raw end over pressed end.

Miter at the points.

6. Turn the bias strip to the right side of the vest, wrapping it over the raw edges to encase them. Press, folding in the miters at the points. Pin the bias strip in place. From the lining side, stitch in the ditch of the seam and remove the pins.

Stitch in the ditch.

7. Apply 1¼"-wide bias strips to each armhole in the same manner as the outer edges, beginning and ending at the lower end of the back armhole, not at the underarm seam (to avoid excess thickness).

8. Turn under and press ¼" along the raw edges of the 1"-wide bias strip. (Use a ½" bias tape maker for speed and ease; see the illustration on page 39).

9. Beginning at the side seam of the vest on the right side, position the bias strip along the stitching on the first bias strip. Miter the points and corners as you pin the second bias strip in place. Overlap the bias strip ends at a side seam and trim the excess bias strip, leaving enough to turn under and press ¼". Stitch close to both long edges of the bias.

10. Add bias-strip trim to the armholes in the manner described in step 9. Position the overlapping ends so that they are not directly on top of the first set of overlapping ends on each armhole.

11. Make four buttonholes in the right vest front; sew buttons in place on the left front.

12. Pop your vest over your favorite T-shirt. Head for the fabric store to show off your new wearable and buy fabric for your next colorful jacket or vest.

About the Author

Judy Murrah learned to sew at an early age from her mother, and she's been exploring this creative medium ever since. With a degree in education and a specialty in art from Southwest Texas State University in her background, she taught her first quilt classes in Houston, Texas, in 1977. Judy teaches her original clothing, decorative, and quilt designs at regional seminars, quilt guilds, and shops throughout the country.

It's not surprising that this prolific designer would find a way to combine her sewing background and her love for patchwork into a book. *Jacket Jazz,* published in May 1993 by That Patchwork Place, was an award-winning bestseller. It was followed by five more titles: *Jacket Jazz Encore, More Jazz from Judy Murrah, Dress Daze, Jazz It Up,* and *In the Studio with Judy Murrah.* Judy has also published patterns, including her *Plain and Fancy Jacket* pattern, a collaboration with

friend and editor, Barbara Weiland, of Jo-Lydia's Attic, and designed a line of fabrics, Jacket Jazz in Another Key, for Clothworks.

Judy's growth as a professional instructor and author has paralleled her responsibilities as Director of Education with Quilts, Inc. Located in Houston, Texas, this organization produces five successful international quilt markets and festivals each year, including the highly acclaimed Houston International Quilt Festival. Judy is responsible for planning and coordinating jam-packed schedules of hands-on classes and lectures by guest instructors for all five events.

Judy is a founding member of the Victoria, Texas, quilt guild and a charter member of the International Quilt Association. She remains active in both organizations. Judy lives in Victoria, Texas, with Tom, her husband of 37 years. They have three adult children, a daughter-in-law, son-in-law, and three grandchildren.

new and bestselling titles from

America's Best-Loved Craft & Hobby Books®
America's Best-Loved Knitting Books®

America's Best-Loved Quilt Books®

NEW RELEASES
Beaded Elegance
Beyond Wool
Burgoyne Surrounded
Clever Quarters
Coffee-Time Quilts
Collage Cards
Crocheted Lace
Dutch Treat
Endless Stars
English Cottage Quilts
Fast-Forward Your Quilting
Garden Stroll, A
Holidays at Home
Knit It Now!
Knits from the Heart
Little Box of Scarves, The
Little Box of Sweaters, The
Machine-Embroidered Quilts
Mad about Plaid!
Quilter's Quick Reference Guide, The
Romantic Quilts
Sensational Settings, Revised Edition
Simple Blessings
Stack a New Deck
Star-Studded Quilts
Stitch and Split Appliqué
Warm Up to Wool
Year of Cats…in Hats!, A

APPLIQUÉ
Appliquilt in the Cabin
Artful Album Quilts
Blossoms in Winter
Garden Party
Shadow Appliqué
Sunbonnet Sue All through the Year

HOLIDAY QUILTS & CRAFTS
Christmas Cats and Dogs
Christmas Delights
Creepy Crafty Halloween
Handcrafted Christmas, A
Hocus Pocus!
Make Room for Christmas Quilts
Welcome to the North Pole

LEARNING TO QUILT
101 Fabulous Rotary-Cut Quilts
Casual Quilter, The
Happy Endings, Revised Edition
Loving Stitches, Revised Edition
More Fat Quarter Quilts
Professional Machine Quilting
Simple Joys of Quilting, The
Your First Quilt Book (or it should be!)

PAPER PIECING
40 Bright and Bold Paper-Pieced Blocks
50 Fabulous Paper-Pieced Stars
Down in the Valley
Easy Machine Paper Piecing
For the Birds
Papers for Foundation Piecing
Quilter's Ark, A
Show Me How to Paper Piece
Traditional Quilts to Paper Piece

QUILTS FOR BABIES & CHILDREN
Easy Paper-Pieced Baby Quilts
Even More Quilts for Baby
More Quilts for Baby
Quilts for Baby
Sweet and Simple Baby Quilts

ROTARY CUTTING/SPEED PIECING
101 Fabulous Rotary-Cut Quilts
365 Quilt Blocks a Year Perpetual
    Calendar
1000 Great Quilt Blocks
Around the Block Again
Around the Block with Judy Hopkins
Clever Quilts Encore
Log Cabin Fever
Once More around the Block
Pairing Up
Strips and Strings
Triangle-Free Quilts
Triangle Tricks

SCRAP QUILTS
Nickel Quilts
Rich Traditions
Scrap Frenzy
Spectacular Scraps
Successful Scrap Quilts

TOPICS IN QUILTMAKING
Asian Elegance
Batiks and Beyond
Bed and Breakfast Quilts
Four Seasons of Quilts
Judy Murrah's Jacket Jackpot
Meadowbrook Quilts
Patchwork Memories
Quilter's Home: Winter, The
Snowflake Follies
Split-Diamond Dazzlers
Time to Quilt
World of Quilts, A

CRAFTS
20 Decorated Baskets
ABCs of Making Teddy Bears, The
Blissful Bath, The
Creating with Paint
Handcrafted Garden Accents
Painted Whimsies
Pretty and Posh
Purely Primitive
Sassy Cats
Stamp in Color
Trashformations

KNITTING & CROCHET
365 Knitting Stitches a Year Perpetual
    Calendar
Basically Brilliant Knits
Classic Knitted Vests
Crochet for Tots
Crocheted Aran Sweaters
Crocheted Socks!
Knits for Children and Their Teddies
Knitted Sweaters for Every Season
Knitted Throws and More
Knitter's Template, A
Simply Beautiful Sweaters for Men
Style at Large
Today's Crochet
Too Cute! Cotton Knits for Toddlers
Treasury of Rowan Knits, A
Ultimate Knitter's Guide, The

Our books are available at
bookstores and your favorite
craft, fabric, and yarn retailers.
If you don't see the title
you're looking for, visit us at
www.martingale-pub.com
or contact us at:

1-800-426-3126

International: 1-425-483-3313
Fax: 1-425-486-7596
Email: info@martingale-pub.com